10-MINUTE IDEAS
FOR EARLY YEARS

DoP

S

Sand and water

Jean Evans

■ Qu⬛⬛⬛⬛⬛ activities f⬛⬛ any time of the day
■ Links to Earl⬛ ⬛⬛⬛⬛⬛e-saving photocopiables

Credits

Author
Jean Evans

Editor
Jane Bishop

Assistant Editor
Aileen Lalor

Series Designer
Anna Oliwa

Designer
Andrea Lewis

Cover Illustration
Craig Cameron/Art Collection

Illustrations
Debbie, Clark

Text © 2004
© 2004 Scholastic Ltd

Designed using Adobe InDesign

Published by Scholastic Ltd
Villiers House
Clarendon Avenue
Leamington Spa
Warwickshire
CV32 5PR

www.scholastic.co.uk

Printed by Bell & Bain

2 3 4 5 6 7 8 9   5 6 7 8 9 0 1 2 3

British Library Cataloguing-in-Publication Data
A catalogue record for this book is available from the British Library.

ISBN 0-439-97142-X

Acknowledgments

The publishers gratefully acknowledge Sally Scott for 'Down by the sea', 'Matching colours', 'Ten tall penguins' and 'This is the way we wash our hands' © 2004, Sally Scott, all previously unpublished (2004, Scholastic Ltd).

Contents

Contents

Introduction

This book is one of a series providing a range of quick and easy to use activities for children in the early years. Each activity has an expected duration of up to ten minutes, although practitioners may wish to extend this if the children become really involved in their play. As most of the activities require little preparation the book will be ideal to 'dip into' when early years practitioners need inspiration. Resources suggested are either everyday objects or those that can be found in most early years settings. The activity ideas can also be used as part of a planned curriculum.

Setting up sand and water areas

Ideally, children should always have access to sand and water play. Make sure that the areas you designate are clearly defined, for example, by using screens. Organise resources so that the children can easily access them and return them after use, for example, hang water aprons and kitchen utensils on hooks, and stick silhouettes made from coloured contact adhesive on shelves, to identify equipment such as funnels and jugs.

Try to colour code plastic equipment for each area, for example, yellow for dry sand, red for wet sand and blue for water, and use the same colour for the silhouettes. Shop around for suitable safe kitchen utensils, for example, plastic sieves, colanders, slotted spoons and potato mashers. Provide a range of natural materials such as shells, cork, small pebbles and conkers, as well as small-world equipment, for exploratory and imaginative play.

Look out for interesting variations on the usual resources, for example, jelly moulds, plastic plumbing pipes and connecting pieces, flexible tubing and plastic plant pots of different sizes. Drill holes of different diameters into a plank, and rest this across the centre of the tray. Encourage the children to use this resource to stand small containers on, or to wedge funnels and tubing into, so that they have both hands free to pour water or sand into them. In addition, a table covered in a towel at the end of the water tray will provide somewhere for children to fill containers with the minimum of spillage.

If it is not possible to have a permanent sand and water area, try using a baby bath on the floor and display equipment on a trolley alongside. Protect the area if necessary with a waterproof sheet, and cover with towels to absorb spills and avoid slipping.

SAND ACTIVITY

WATER ACTIVITY

Health and safety

Always have a small mop and plastic mop bucket, or a dustpan, brush and small bucket, at hand so that children can clean up their own spills.

Remember to change water after each session and to sieve sand and replace it regularly. Emphasise that the children should not drink the water or put sand in their mouths or near their eyes, and ensure that they always wash and dry their hands after sand play.

Consider the needs of all the children in the group and adapt resources if necessary, for example, by lowering the height of the water tray or using utensils with easy grip handles. Always check for allergies when adding any colouring, perfumes or soap.

How the book is organised

This book is organised into six activity chapters, one for each Area of Learning (*Curriculum Guidance for the Foundation Stage* (QCA)). Within each chapter there are ten activity pages: five for sand play and five for water play, identified by the symbols on the left. The five sand activities have a balance of dry and wet sand ideas, as well as some suggestions for outdoor sandpits. Most of the activities take place in sand and water trays to encourage practitioners to extend the range of learning experiences in these play areas. Because of this, the group size is generally around four children. However, the importance of sand and water as learning resources cannot be underestimated and so the book also includes activities focusing on daily routines and other play areas.

Photocopiable pages have been included as a stimulating start to an activity, or as a follow-up to extend ideas and play. There are stories, poems and songs linked to the activities, as well as child-centred ideas involving games, matching and cutting and sticking, directly linked to the activities.

Planning for the Foundation Stage

This book aims to provide ideas to cover as many of the Early Learning Goals as possible, and every cluster of goals, or group of goals with a similar focus, is visited at least once. Each activity is linked to a particular Stepping Stone and Early Learning Goal to assist practitioners with planning. Activities include examples from each band of Stepping Stones so that practitioners can meet the needs of individuals as they progress through these Stepping Stones towards the Early Learning Goals. The result is a balance of learning opportunities across the whole Foundation Stage curriculum.

Assessing the activities

The activities in this book are generally limited to four children. Working with such a small group within a designated play area provides an ideal opportunity for you to make close observations of individuals. Each activity page includes suggestions for supporting younger children and extending older children as they take part. These suggestions can also provide useful indicators when assessing children. If a child manages the activity without support, for example, or enjoys the challenge of the extension ideas, then that child has achieved the given Stepping Stone. If a child still needs support, then that child has not yet reached the given level.

Personal, social and emotional development

The activities in this chapter encourage children to be confident in approaching new experiences, be considerate of other people's feelings, views and needs in group work and to be independent when working alone.

Sand mosaics

LEARNING OBJECTIVES
STEPPING STONE
Have a positive approach to new experiences.

EARLY LEARNING GOAL
Continue to be interested, excited and motivated to learn.

GROUP SIZE
Four children.

What you need
Floor and wall tiles with mosaic patterns; dry sand; four jugs; six shallow plastic trays; small pebbles; shells; card; scissors; felt pens.

What to do
Pass around the tiles and discuss their uses. Invite the children to trace along the lines of the patterns with a finger. Talk about whether the lines are straight or curved. Identify any definite shapes such as triangles, squares and circles.

Suggest that the children try to make their own mosaic patterns in the shallow trays. Supply each child with a tray, and a jug of dry sand to pour into the middle of it.

Encourage the children to smooth out the sand with their fingers to form a flat surface, on which to create their mosaic patterns.

Use the remaining two trays to display the pebbles and shells in the centre of the table.

Invite the children to choose pebbles and shells from the trays and arrange them in patterns on the dry sand in their trays. Encourage them to try different combinations, explaining that they can return shells and pebbles to the centre trays and choose different ones as often as they wish.

When the children are satisfied with their creations help them to make a name label from card. Display their patterns with the labels on a table top for others to admire.

Support and extension
Simply supply younger children with trays of sand, pebbles and shells to explore freely, rather than suggest they try to copy patterns. Encourage older children to copy their patterns onto paper.

HOME LINKS
Suggest that parents and carers create mosaic patterns on the beach with their children using pebbles and shells. Ask parents and carers to involve their children in visits to a DIY store to look at mosaic tiles and wallpaper patterns.

Further ideas
■ Push pebbles and shells into flat squares of wet clay or plaster of Paris to create textured mosaic tiles.
■ Print patterns with sponge shapes using thick brightly-coloured paint.
■ Cut geometrical shapes from coloured paper and glue them to card to create mosaic pictures.
■ Explore pictures of patterns found in Islamic art and try to recreate them.

Happy Birthday to you!

What you need
Birthday wrapping paper; imitation present; pictures of birthday cakes; photographs of the children's birthday cakes; cake candles and decorations; birthday cards; sand tray or outdoor sand-pit; wet sand; shells; pebbles; small twigs; sand tools; buckets; bowls; recipe books.

Preparation
Invite parents and carers to loan birthday cards and photographs of their children's cakes and parties. Make a display by covering a table with wrapping paper and standing the open recipe books, photographs, cards, present, candles and cake decorations on top.

What to do
Encourage the children to explore the display and talk about their experiences of birthdays. Can they remember having a special cake?

Suggest creating birthday cakes in wet sand using buckets and bowls to mould cake shapes, and pebbles and shells for decoration.

As the children make their cakes discuss family celebrations. Do they have special cakes to celebrate other events? Suggest using the twigs as candles and talk about how many should be put on each cake.

Sing 'Happy Birthday' to a chosen doll before pretending to blow out the candles on the sand cakes.

Support and extension
Help younger children's sense of belonging to the group by asking them to help you to make one big cake for a chosen doll, using wet sand. Encourage older children to make comparisons between the sizes of the cakes they make, and to count twig candles up to ten.

Further ideas
■ Put cups, jugs and a teapot into dry sand and encourage the children to pretend to pour out cups of tea.
■ Celebrate a special birthday or event by baking and icing small sponge cakes together.
■ Talk about special events related to the different cultures of the children in your group. Make sand cakes to celebrate events such as christenings and weddings, and use appropriate pastry cutters to mould sand shapes during festivals, for example, heart shapes on St Valentine's Day or crescent moons during the Chinese Moon Festival.

Anyone for tea?

What you need
Shallow sand tray; dry sand; four dolls dressed in party clothes; a dolls' tea set; table cloth; natural materials such as pine cones, sycamore keys, conkers and leaves; small bowls.

Preparation
Stand the sand tray on a washable floor surface and arrange the natural materials in separate bowls around it. Leave the cloth and tea set nearby.

What to do
Show the children the dolls in their party clothes and explain that you would like them to help you to make a party tea for the dolls. Ask them to choose a doll each to look after. Spread out the cloth and sit the dolls around it.

Show the children the tea set and the natural materials and encourage them to use the materials to make pretend sandwiches, cakes and other party food. Arrange the foods on the plates and put them on the cloth for the dolls to enjoy. Talk about the importance of sharing and invite the children to share the pretend food equally between the dolls.

Suggest that the children fill the teapot, jug and sugar bowl with dry sand and pretend to pour out cups of tea for the dolls. Emphasise the importance of taking turns at filling the teapot and pouring the sand into the cups.

Shake any spilt sand back into the tray at the end of the activity.

Support and extension
Younger children will enjoy simply filling and emptying the cups, jugs and teapot with dry sand. Praise them for sharing the resources and for taking turns as they do so. Encourage older children to count out food items and measure dry sand into cups to ensure the dolls have equal quantities.

LEARNING OBJECTIVES
STEPPING STONE
Seek out others to share experiences.

EARLY LEARNING GOAL
Work as part of a group or class, taking turns and sharing fairly.

GROUP SIZE
Four children.

Further ideas
■ Invite the children to make sandwiches and mix up some fruit juice for an outdoor picnic. Emphasise the importance of taking turns to hand out food and discuss how the children might share out the juice equally.
■ Take the tea set to the dough table and create some dough food to put out on plates.

HOME LINKS
Invite parents and carers to a picnic prepared and served by the children to emphasise the need to take turns and share fairly.

Mary, Mary

What you need
Small sand tray; wet sand; foil; card; scissors; cockle shells; wooden dolly pegs; fabric scraps; tape; string; felt pens; wool; PVA glue; small stones; recycled materials such as wood offcuts, cotton reels and small boxes; shallow storage boxes; knowledge of the nursery rhyme 'Mary, Mary Quite Contrary' (Traditional).

Preparation
Ask a small group of children to make some 'pretty maids' from wooden pegs. Dress the pegs in fabric scraps tied or taped into place, add features with a felt pen and glue on scraps of wool to represent hair. Create silver bells by cutting card into bell shapes and pressing silver foil tightly over it.

What to do
Arrange the small stones, silver bells, cockle shells and pretty maids in separate shallow boxes on a table, alongside the sand tray. Provide the box of recycled materials to create additional garden features.

Sing the rhyme 'Mary, Mary, Quite Contrary' and encourage the children to talk about what Mary's garden might look like. Suggest that the children make comparisons with their own experience of gardens. Suggest creating Mary's garden in the sand tray from the resources.

Create paths from small stones for visitors to walk around and arrange the silver bells, cockle shells and pretty maids in rows along them.

Ask the children what else they would like to include, for example, seats for visitors, a bird table or a pond. Look through the recycled materials for suitable resources to create these features.

Support and extension
Present younger children with the resources and let them play freely with them in the sand. Sing the rhyme as they are playing, pointing to the items mentioned. Introduce small-world characters so that older children can make up stories as they play.

Further ideas
■ Transform wet sand into a topic related environment such as a jungle, desert or lunar landscape using recycled material and small-world equipment.
■ Dramatise other nursery rhymes using small-world characters in wet sand, for example, create a wall for Humpty Dumpty to fall off or a hill for Jack and Jill to fall down.

Rangoli patterns

What you need
Pictures of rangoli patterns from information books; copy of the photocopiable sheet 'Rangoli patterns' on page 67; squares of card; PVA glue; glue spreaders; coloured sand or dry sand mixed with powder paint.

Preparation
If you have no pictures of rangoli patterns, create symmetrical drawings using geometric shapes on squares of card. Alternatively, use the photocopiable page as an example.

What to do
Show the children the pictures of rangoli patterns or geometric shapes and talk about them. Can they recognise any definite shapes within the patterns such as circles or triangles?

Explain how rangoli patterns are drawn at the entrances to Hindu homes during Divali to welcome the goddess Lakshmi.
Suggest that the children create some rangoli patterns of their own using coloured sand.

Supply each child with a square of card and demonstrate how to divide it into four smaller squares or triangles by drawing two lines from corner to corner or across the middle, so that the lines cross in the centre.

Ask the children to paint over the lines with PVA glue using a glue spreader and then suggest that they draw shapes with glue within the sections of the card.

Invite the children to sprinkle the coloured sand over the whole of their cards and then shake off the excess.

Allow the sand patterns to dry and then display them.

Support and extension
Encourage younger children to create very simple patterns by making blobs of glue all over the card and then shaking sand over it using a flour dredger. Invite older children to recreate their rangoli patterns on a hard surface outdoors using coloured chalks.

Further ideas
■ Introduce the children to traditional patterns on fabrics from other cultures and invite them to recreate similar designs using paint or felt pens.
■ Introduce the children to stencilling using commercially produced stencils or create your own by drawing a design on card and cutting it out.
■ Use face paints to create mendhi patterns on the children's hands.
■ Cut out and colour the rangoli patterns on the photocopiable sheet on page 67, then display them.

LEARNING OBJECTIVES
STEPPING STONE
Have an awareness of, and show interest and enjoyment in, cultural and religious differences.

EARLY LEARNING GOAL
Understand that people have different needs, views, cultures and beliefs, that need to be treated with respect.

GROUP SIZE
Up to six children.

HOME LINKS
Invite parents and carers to bring in traditional clothing associated with their own cultures and explore patterns and designs.

Warm and comfortable

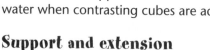

LEARNING OBJECTIVES
STEPPING STONE
Display high levels of involvement in activities.

EARLY LEARNING GOAL
Maintain attention, concentrate, and sit quietly when appropriate.

GROUP SIZE
Four children.

What you need
Water tray; warm water; two packets of jelly in contrasting colours; measuring jug; large spoon; kettle.

Preparation
Check for food allergies and intolerances.

What to do
Put some warm water into a water tray and invite the children to put their hands into it. Is it hot, warm or cold? Encourage the children to talk about their experiences of water at different temperatures and discuss the dangers of very hot water.

Show the children one of the packets of jelly and pass around the tablet for the children to feel and smell. Do they notice a pattern on the top? Explain that the tablet is divided into small cubes so that it can be broken up easily.

Invite the children to try to separate the tablet into cubes. Discuss how the sticky jelly stretches and help the children if necessary. Share out the cubes among them, making sure everyone has an equal amount.

Ask what they think will happen to the cubes if they drop them into the water. Will they drop straight to the bottom or float on the surface? Take turns to drop one into the water.

Look at the cubes lying at the bottom of the water. Is anything happening to them? Invite the children to swish the water around very gently and then look again. Can they see the cubes starting to dissolve?

Encourage the children to play freely for a while before introducing the second jelly tablet. What happens to the colour of the water when contrasting cubes are added?

Support and extension
Encourage younger children to play freely with a mixture of set jelly and warm water, rather than asking them to break jelly tablets into cubes. Ask older children to think of words to describe how the jelly looks, feels and smells and scribe these for them onto a large sheet of paper.

Further ideas
■ Make up a jelly together to enjoy at snack time, introducing appropriate vocabulary such as 'set', 'dissolve', 'solid' and 'liquid' as you do so.
■ Add drops of food colouring one by one to the water and look at what happens to it.

Spiders and worms

What you need
Water tray; warm water; spaghetti; large pan; red food colouring; plastic spiders.

Preparation
Check for food allergies and intolerances. Cook some spaghetti in a large pan with a drop of red food colouring so that it turns pink.

What to do
Invite the children to put their hands into warm water in a water tray and talk about how it feels. Do they prefer warm or cold water?

Ask the children to turn around and close their eyes. Add the pink spaghetti and swirl it around to that it is evenly spread in the water.

Invite the children to open their eyes and look into the water. What has happened to it? Encourage them to play with the new mixture and talk about their feelings. Do they enjoy handling warm gooey spaghetti worms?

Suggest that the children close their eyes again before adding the plastic spiders and covering them with spaghetti so that they are hidden from view. Invite the children to look at the mixture again. Does it look any different? Encourage them to explore it thoroughly. What can they find?

Talk about the children's feelings about the spiders and spaghetti worms. Do any of them feel afraid? Reassure them that they are 'pretend' and talk in general about things that make them frightened.

Support and extension
Omit the spiders with very young children and concentrate on the pleasure of handling the warm soft spaghetti mixture. Invite older children to create a 'scary potion' with dark blue spaghetti and plastic insects of their choice. As they play, encourage them to discuss their fears and anxieties.

Further ideas
■ Put a large stone into the water with a tiny character sitting on top of it and sing the nursery rhyme 'Little Miss Muffet' (Traditional)
■ Tie a plastic spider to some string and drop it through a length of plastic piping. Hold the piping upright in the spaghetti mixture and sing 'Incy Wincy Spider' (Traditional) pulling the spider up and out of the pipe as you do so.

LEARNING OBJECTIVES
STEPPING STONE
Express needs and feelings in appropriate ways

EARLY LEARNING GOAL
Respond to significant experiences showing a range of feelings when appropriate.

GROUP SIZE
Four children.

HOME LINKS
Suggest that parents and carers use food colouring to add interest to pasta dishes at home, for example, creating pink spaghetti worms or green pasta grass.

Out on the ocean waves

What you need
Large water tray; blue and green food colouring; small-world characters; toy boats; small rocks; shells; green Cellophane; bubble wrap; small corks; string.

Preparation
Check for food allergies and intolerances.

What to do
Talk to the children about their experiences of visits to the seaside. What did they most enjoy doing?

Suggest creating the sea in the water tray for small-world characters to enjoy. Try to recreate the colour of the sea by gradually adding drops of blue and green food colouring. Make seaweed from long strips of green cellophane floating in the water. Drop in some shells and small rocks.

Discuss the fun and dangers of paddling and swimming in the sea and suggest that the children work together to create buoyancy aids for the small-world characters from bubble wrap or small corks.

Allow time for the children to play freely with the resources, with the characters taking imaginary boat trips and swimming in the sea. Interact to encourage the children to make group decisions about the direction of play.

Support and extension
Set up the scene for younger children beforehand so that they can play freely alongside one another, watching actions and beginning to relate to one another. Encourage older children to work in pairs to support one another, for example, to design a boat from recycled materials.

Further ideas
■ Work as a group to create a desert island in the middle of the water, deciding together what materials will be most suitable. Will anything be growing there? Make up stories about small-world characters sailing or swimming to and from the island.

■ Set up a 'seaside' paddling pool outdoors and encourage older children to help younger children to prepare for and enjoy the experience.

Bath time

What you need
Two bowls or baby baths; two dolls with hair, fully dressed; shampoo; bubble bath; soap; bath toys; three towels; two children's waterproof aprons; sponges, loofahs and cloths; jug; clean clothes for dolls.

Preparation
Set up three tables, one for each child to work at and one for accessories. Arrange the washing accessories on a towel on one of the tables and invite the children to wear aprons.

Before the activity, check for allergies to any of the products used.

What to do
Take the children to the table to look at the washing accessories and talk about their own experiences of washing and having a bath. Have they ever used any of the accessories?

Suggest that they bath two of the dolls from the home area. Invite the children to choose a doll and undress it.

Talk about how much water to put in the bath and what might be a suitable temperature. Explain why very hot or very cold water would be unsuitable.

As the children bath their dolls talk about their choices of accessories. Emphasise the importance of handling the dolls gently and make comparisons with caring for small babies.

Once the dolls are bathed and dried ask the children to choose clean clothes for them before returning them to the home area.

Support and extension
Provide younger children with fewer choices and ensure that the fastenings on the doll's clothes are manageable. Talk to older children about caring for living things in general, for example, bathing and grooming pets regularly.

■ ■

Further ideas
■ Mount a copy of the photocopiable sheet 'Time for a bath' on page 68 on card and colour and cut out the pictures. Discuss how all the items would be used. Invite the children to pick out the pictures associated with washing and bathing.
■ Introduce festivals associated with caring for living things and the environment, for example, the Israeli tree-planting festival of Tu b'Shevat, World Environment Day or the Buddhist festival of Wesak.
■ Set up a role-play pet shop to encourage the children to care for soft toys and to discuss accessories that are needed to ensure their welfare.

LEARNING OBJECTIVES
STEPPING STONE
Show care and concern for others, for living things and the environment.

EARLY LEARNING GOAL
Consider the consequences of their words and actions for themselves and others.

GROUP SIZE
Two children.

HOME LINKS
Invite a parent or carer to bath a young baby while the children watch.

Splat those germs

What you need

Copy of the song 'This is how we wash our hands' on the photocopiable sheet on page 69; soap (check for allergies); nailbrushes; paper towels in a towel dispenser; hand basins; bin; paint; aprons.

What to do

Sing the song on the photocopiable sheet with the children, adding actions as indicated.

Ask the children when they wash their hands and why. Invite them to wear aprons. Encourage them to have fun covering their hands with paint and then suggest that they wash it off again.

Take the children to the cloakroom area and demonstrate how to put the plug in a hand basin and turn the tap on and off. Explain how water comes along pipes into the taps and discuss how much water should be put in the hand basin.

Demonstrate how to wash hands thoroughly using soap, and a nailbrush if necessary, and then rinse them in clean water before pulling out the plug. Pull a paper towel from the dispenser and dry the hands before disposing of the towel in the bin.

Ask the children to follow your example and wash their hands until all of the paint has disappeared.

LEARNING OBJECTIVES

STEPPING STONE

Take initiatives and manage developmentally appropriate tasks.

EARLY LEARNING GOAL

Dress and undress independently and manage their own personal hygiene.

GROUP SIZE

Up to six children.

Support and extension

Help younger children with the washing process, examining their hands to ensure that they are thoroughly clean. Talk to older children about how germs carried on dirty hands can cause them to feel ill.

Further ideas

■ If children do not have direct access to cloakroom facilities, provide them with clean water in a bowl, soap and paper towels so that they can wash their hands when necessary.

■ Explore different types of soap such as liquid soap, soapflakes and bars of soap. Which do the children think is best for hand washing? Try washing dirty hands in warm and cold water. Which is most successful?

HOME LINKS

Send home a copy of the hand washing song and ask parents and carers to continue to emphasise the importance of thorough hand washing at home.

■ Make towels from squares of different materials, such as towelling, plastic, paper, cotton fabric and wool, and investigate which is most successful for drying wet hands.

Communication, language and literacy

This chapter suggests ideas to help children learn how to respond to simple instructions, pay attention at story time and to interact with others. Children will begin to link sounds and letters, naming and sounding the letters of the alphabet.

Lost in the woods

What you need
Copy of the story 'Lost in the woods' on the photocopiable sheet on page 70; sand tray; wet sand; two small-world dogs; green tissue; wood offcuts; twigs; thick card; scissors.

What to do
Read the story 'Lost in the woods' to the children. Discuss how the two puppies resolve their disagreements and talk about arguments the children might have experienced. How did they react?

Suggest creating scenes from the story in the sand tray. Discuss how to create the landscape, for example, making the fence from card, the grassy field from tissue scraps, the bumpy bridge from wood offcuts, the big hill from sand and the deep wood from twigs.

Work together on the landscape, using the children's ideas and making suggestions to extend them if necessary.

Introduce the model dogs and encourage the children to re-enact the story and make up stories of their own.

Support and extension
Rather than read the story, simplify the activity for younger children by encouraging them to explore the resources and helping them to decide upon the direction the play takes, for example, by asking 'Shall we make a big hill in the sand? Can you help the dogs to climb up it? What else shall we do?'. Give older children more choices to encourage them to make decisions, for example, asking whether to use wood offcuts or blocks for the bridge.

Further ideas
■ Re-enact favourite stories such as 'The Enormous Turnip' (Traditional) in the sand tray, using props chosen by the children after discussion together.
■ Let the children pretend to be the puppies in the story and follow their journey using large apparatus. Involve the children in deciding about how to set up the equipment.

LEARNING OBJECTIVES
STEPPING STONE
Initiate conversation, attend to and take account of what others say, and use talk to resolve disagreements.

EARLY LEARNING GOAL
Interact with others, negotiating plans and activities and taking turns in conversation.

GROUP SIZE
Up to four children.

HOME LINKS
Send home copies of the story and invite parents and carers to re-enact it with their children using toys as the dogs and everyday items, such as cushions and stools, to re-create their journey.

Find a match

What you need
Sand tray; dry sand; two seaside buckets; two sets of up to ten matching
plastic letters; minute sand timer.

Preparation
Choose up to ten plastic letters that the children are most familiar with and
put one set in each seaside bucket.

What to do
Show the children the two buckets of letters. Tip the letters from one of the
buckets into a tray of dry sand and ask the children to hide them.

Suggest that the children take turns to pull a letter out of the second bucket
and show it to the others. Can they say the letter sound? Do they know the
name of the letter?

Set the sand timer going and ask a child to pull a letter from the bucket and
then find the matching hidden letter in the sand before the sand runs out. If
the letter is not discovered, reset the timer and ask the other children to help
this time.

Continue until all hidden letters are found and matched.

Support and extension
Focus on a few familiar letters at first and gradually increase them according
to the age and stage of development of younger children. Encourage older
children to find an object hidden in the sand with the same initial sound as the
letter they pull from the bucket.

Further ideas
■ Vary the game by putting numbers, small everyday items or plastic bricks
of different sizes and colours in the bucket and hiding the matching objects
in the sand.
■ Put the letters under a cloth and take away one at a time without the
children seeing. Invite the children to say either the sound or the name of the
letter that is missing.

Dinosaur worlds

What you need
Reference books about dinosaurs; copy of the story 'The biggest dinosaur' on the photocopiable sheet on page 71; sand tray or outdoor sand-pit; wet sand; plastic dinosaurs including several tyrannosaurus rex, a diplodocus, a stegosaurus and a pterodactyl; blue fabric; twigs; small rocks and pebbles.

What to do
Look at the books about dinosaurs. Look at the models too, and talk about their features.

Read the story 'The biggest dinosaur', pausing at appropriate points to ask the children how Terry the dinosaur might solve his problem.

Suggest that the children create a dinosaur world in wet sand. Encourage them to use small rocks, pebbles and twigs to create the landscape in the sand tray or outdoor sand-pit.

Add model dinosaurs, looking in the reference books if necessary to discover their names. Leave the children to play freely with the world they have created.

Suggest re-enacting the story using the children's landscape. Build caves in the sand and arrange twigs in front of one of them to represent the trees in the story. Ask appropriate questions about what happened next to encourage the children to tell the story in the correct sequence.

Support and extension
Set up the landscape for younger children to play freely with the dinosaurs. Make suggestions to extend their imaginary ideas. Encourage older children to think of different endings for the story and invite them to take turns to re-enact their stories while the others watch.

Further ideas
■ Create landscapes, such as a polar or lunar environment, for small-world play using papier mâché in a builder's tray. Allow the landscape to dry before painting and varnishing it. Encourage children to invent stories using small-world characters.
■ Read *Harry and the Bucketful of Dinosaurs* by Ian Whybrow (Puffin) and encourage the children to retell the story using model dinosaurs in a bucket and thinking of new endings.

Stranded on an island

What you need
Copy of the photocopiable sheet 'Letter home' on page 72; sand or water tray; wet sand; driftwood; moss; twigs; shells; small rocks; pebbles; small-world character and wild animals; toy boat; film spool container; paper; pencils.

What to do
Read the copy of the letter on the photocopiable sheet to the children. Who do they think might have written it and why? Choose a name for the writer and write it in the space provided.

Suggest creating an island and making up a story about the letter writer.

Put a sand or water tray on the floor with some wet sand in the middle. Invite the children to make the sand into the shape of an island.

Suggest that the children add appropriate resources, for example, make trees from twigs, add clumps of moss 'bushes', arrange rocks among the trees and create a beach from pebbles and shells.

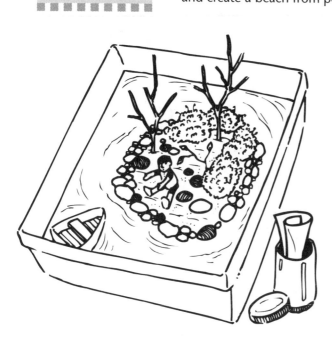

Put the small-world character in the boat along with a film spool container, paper scraps and pencil. Suggest that the lost character decides to land on the island.

Talk about sending messages. Can the children think of ways of sending messages. Introduce the words 'telephone', 'mobile phone', 'letter', 'postcard', 'email'. Which of these options could the stranded character use?

Talk about what might be written or drawn on the message and scribe for the children using paper and pencil. Fold up the finished message and put it in the container. Put the lid on tightly. Roll the container into the imaginary water.

Encourage the children to use small-world equipment to make up stories about who picks up the message and rescues the stranded character. Supply lots of paper scraps to enable the children to continue the activity, writing their own messages.

Support and extension
Encourage younger children to make paper flags to fly on the island with their individual marks on them. Suggest that older children write their names on the messages.

Further ideas
■ Send messages in other ways, for example, posting a letter or sending a greetings card or e-mail.
■ Include some resources for writing messages in role-play and in small-world play areas.

Making our mark

What you need
Small shallow trays; dry sand; twigs; chopsticks; lollipop sticks; straws; plastic letters; thick cardboard strips; writing tools such as pencils, felt pens, chalk and crayons.

Preparation
Make some cardboard strips, the same width as the trays, to be used to flatten the surface of the sand.

What to do
Put a small amount of dry sand in each tray and invite the children to spread evenly it over the surface.

Explain that these are magic trays as the children can draw and write on them and then make the writing disappear.

Invite the children to explore the sand and make marks freely using fingers and thumbs. Demonstrate how to smooth the sand over by using the cardboard strip.

Introduce the plastic letters and suggest that the children try to write them in the sand using a finger.

Look at some pencils, crayons, chalk and felt pens and discuss what they are used for. Suggest that the children try writing in the sand with different things, and introduce the twigs, chopsticks, lollipop sticks and straws.

Explore the newly introduced resources freely.

Support and extension
Give younger children twigs to create patterns in dry sand in the sand tray initially so that they can make larger movements. Introduce older children's name cards to the table so that they can try to write their names.

Further ideas
■ Invite the children to roll out some clay to form a flat tile, and use the activity resources to write their names or make patterns in it. Either bake the tile or allow it to harden in the air before painting and varnishing.
■ Suggest that the children write their names on thick card in glue with a glue spreader and then sprinkle dry sand over the surface. Shake off the excess sand to form a textured name card.

LEARNING OBJECTIVES
STEPPING STONE
Engage in activities requiring hand-eye coordination.

EARLY LEARNING GOAL
Use a pencil and hold it correctly to form recognisable letters, most of which are correctly formed.

GROUP SIZE
Up to six children.

HOME LINKS
Send home a recipe for playdough and suggest that parents and carers encourage their children to make marks in the dough using kitchen utensils, such as forks and whisks.

A splash of colour

LEARNING OBJECTIVES
STEPPING STONE
Listen to others in one-to-one/small groups when conversation interests them.

EARLY LEARNING GOAL
Sustain attentive listening, responding to what they have heard by relevant comments, questions or actions.

GROUP SIZE
Up to four children.

What you need
A copy of the song 'Matching colours' on the photocopiable sheet on page 73; water tray; water; food colouring; plastic resources in matching colours.

Preparation
Give the children a coloured bucket each and invite them to look around and find plastic resources of the same colour to collect.

What to do
Sing the first verse of the song 'Matching colours' and ask the children to point to something red. Continue to make up verses, asking the children to point to a different colour for each one. Discuss the things the children point to, praising them for their contributions and for listening attentively to others.

Do the children have a favourite colour? Can they say why? Praise those who respond with relevant comments and further questions.

Show the children the full buckets and invite them to choose one to empty into the water for the session.

Will it be possible to make the colour of the water match the resources? Look at the food colouring available and choose what to use. Drop in the colour gradually. Is it possible to mix colours, for example, to create green? Once the children are happy with the colour they have mixed, invite them to tip the contents of the bucket into the tray and play freely with them.

Support and extension
Present younger children with ready coloured water and matching resources and talk about the colour as they play, to reinforce their experiences. Ask more challenging questions to encourage older children to respond with relevant comments, questions and actions.

Further ideas
■ Invite a large group of children to sit in a circle and then alter the words of the song 'Matching colours' to:

'Who is wearing red today?
Red today, red today?
Who is wearing red today?
Stand up and show us'.

■ Invent different verses to suit the clothes the children are wearing.
■ Talk about the colours of a rainbow and invite the children to paint a large rainbow to form the background to a display about favourite colours.

HOME LINKS
Ask parents and carers to talk to their children about different colours in the world around them.

What a problem!

What you need
Water tray; warm water; plastic screw-top bottles of varying sizes.

Preparation
Fill the water tray with warm water so that there is a good depth for the activity.

What to do
Show the children the selection of bottles and ask what they think will happen if they are put in the water.

Invite them to choose a bottle to drop in the water. Which way does it float – upright or sideways? Suggest that the children push their chosen bottles down under the water. What do they notice? Talk about how the water pressure tries to push the bottle up again.

Can the children think of a way to make the bottles stay under the water when they stop holding them? Suggest taking the top off the bottle and letting some water enter. Discuss what happens.

Try half-filling the bottle and putting the top back on before dropping the bottle into the water. Does it still float? What happens if the bottle is full?

Encourage the children to play freely with the bottles, putting different amounts of water in before screwing the tops back on.

Invite the children to discuss their observations. Can they make any conclusions about why empty bottles float and full bottles sink?

Support and extension
Leave bottles in the water tray with varying amounts of water in them, from empty to full, and encourage younger children to explore them freely. Give a commentary as the children are busy to encourage them to think about their observations.

Challenge older children to explain the sequence of actions needed to make a bottle sink and encourage them to demonstrate the activity to younger children.

Further ideas
■ Pose the children further problems, such as counting how many small-world characters can sit in a toy boat before it sinks. Invite them to talk about their conclusions.

■ Suggest that the children try to make buoyancy aids for small-world characters using different materials, such as bubble wrap, sponge, paper or towelling, and then discuss the success of their investigations.

Shiny shells

What you need
Books and posters about the seaside; clear shallow plastic bowl; selection of shells; table of child height; yellow cloth; water.

Preparation
A few days before the activity create an interactive display by hanging some seaside posters behind a table draped in a yellow cloth. Half-fill the bowl with water, put in the shells and stand it on the cloth in the middle of the table. Arrange the seaside books around it. Encourage the children to explore the display freely.

What to do
Talk to the children about the display. What do they think it is about?

Look at the posters together and then take some of the books into the story corner to share. Discuss the pictures and any recollections the children have of seaside visits.

Invite the children to sit in a circle and put the bowl of shells in the middle. Explain that these are special shells that will remind them of the seaside.

Suggest that the children take turns to close their eyes and put a hand in the bowl to pull out a shell. While their eyes are closed ask them to talk about how the shell feels. What can they see in their minds? Can they remember any special seaside sounds or smells?

Support and extension
Put shells into the water tray and join younger children as they play with them. Use seaside-related vocabulary to help them to recall past experiences. Encourage older children to make a 'seaside memories' book by scribing their comments for them as they make their recollections. Invite them to illustrate the book.

Further ideas
■ Pass around a large shell and invite the children to put it to their ears and listen to the sound of the sea. Does it remind them of running on the sand and paddling in the water?
■ Use sensory props to evoke memories, for example, make some soup together and talk about past experiences of favourite hot meals or helping to cook at home.

LEARNING OBJECTIVES
STEPPING STONE
Use talk, actions and objects to recall and relive past experiences.

EARLY LEARNING GOAL
Use language to imagine and recreate roles and experiences.

GROUP SIZE
Up to six children.

Fishing for sounds

What you need
Sponge or plastic lower case letters; four small fishing nets; small objects with initial sounds to correspond with the letters, such as a hat, toy dog, ball and toy cow; towel.

What to do
Put the letters into a tray of water and arrange the objects and the fishing nets on a towel on a table alongside.

Invite the children to choose a fishing net and take turns to fish for a letter. When a child catches a letter invite him or her to say the sound and then to look on the table to find something starting with that sound. If the child needs support, suggest that the other children help. Never tell a child a suggestion is 'wrong', but encourage another try, giving lots of praise for taking part.

Once an object has been matched with the letter, put the letter beside it and invite the next child to begin fishing for another letter.

Continue until all the letters have been caught and matched up.

Support and extension
Put a few each of just two letters of contrasting shapes in the water for younger children to catch, for example, 'o' and 'l' and invite them to put them alongside the same letter on the table rather than match them to an object. Say the sound of the letter each time as the child puts the letter on the table. Encourage older children to catch the letters to spell out three letter words corresponding to the objects on the table, such as 'hat' or 'dog'.

Further ideas
■ Plan the same activity using numerals rather than letters and match them to groups with the same number of objects.
■ Reverse the activity by putting the plastic objects into the water and inviting the children to catch them and match them to their initial letter on the table.

LEARNING OBJECTIVES
STEPPING STONE
Hear and say the initial sounds in words.

EARLY LEARNING GOAL
Hear and say the initial sounds in words.

GROUP SIZE
Four children.

HOME LINKS
Encourage parents and carers to play 'I spy' to raise children's awareness of initial letter sounds.

Sticky names

What you need
Four shallow trays; cornflour; water; jug; spoon; lollipop sticks; children's name cards; powder paint; small bowls; white paper.

What to do
Hold up the children's name cards one by one and invite them to put up a hand when they recognise their name.

Talk about how the children write their names on their work using a pencil and explain that you are going to have fun together writing their names in different ways.

Invite a child to half-fill a jug with some cornflour and another child to add two of three tablespoons of powder paint. Finally, choose someone to add water slowly until the mixture is thick and creamy.

Provide each child with a shallow tray and pass around the jug asking them to pour some of the cornflour mixture into their tray to cover the surface.

Suggest that they try to write their names in the mixture. What happens to the marks they make? Try writing with the lollipop sticks. Is the writing any clearer? Use the word 'disappear' and talk about whether the children's writing disappears when they use a pencil to write on paper.

Suggest trying to make marks with the mixture on paper and pour some into small bowls. Take away the trays and provide the children with pieces of paper.

Can they see the marks they have made with the lollipop sticks and cornflour mixture?

Allow time to explore the resources freely.

Support and extension
Younger children will enjoy simply making marks in the cornflour mixture with a lollipop stick and watching them disappear. Encourage older children to try writing their names using everyday objects, such as sticks, feathers or straws, dipped into paint.

Further ideas
■ Explore writing from different cultures and try to copy some of the marks.
■ Provide children with washing-up liquid containers filled with water and suggest that they squeeze them to make marks on a hard outdoor surface.

LEARNING OBJECTIVES
STEPPING STONE
Use writing as a means of recording and communicating.

EARLY LEARNING GOAL
Write their own names and other things.

GROUP SIZE
Four children.

HOME LINKS
Encourage parents and carers to provide their children with a wide range of mark-making materials to explore.

Mathematical development

These activities will encourage children to count and to begin to use mathematical language in play. The chapter suggests ideas to introduce children to positional language and number names and familiarise them with discussing shapes, arrangements and simple patterns.

Stepping stones

What you need
Dry sand; sand tray; cardboard cube; paper; coloured sticky paper; scissors; ten flat pebbles; thin paintbrush; white paint; four small-world animals; a small box.

Preparation
Paint numbers from one to ten on the pebbles using white paint. Cover a cardboard cube, such as a tissue box, in white paper. Create twelve circles from coloured sticky paper and glue these to the cube faces so that there are two faces with each number of circles from one to three, and that the same numbers are opposite one another.

What to do
Show the children the numbered pebbles and invite them to arrange them in order in the dry sand. Which number will they start with? Take turns to place the pebbles on the surface so that they are evenly spread.

Position the box at the end of the line of pebbles, next to the number ten. Introduce the small-world animals and ask the children to choose one to play with. Explain that the animals are going to jump across the pebbles, starting at number one, to reach their shelter next to number ten.

Show the children the dice you have created and count the number of spots on each face together. Explain that you would like the children to take turns to throw the dice and count the number of spots on the upturned face. They can then make their animal jump across the same number of pebbles.

The game will continue until all of the animals have reached the shelter.

Support and extension
Make the dice with three sets of one spot and three sets of two for younger children. Replace spots with numerals or, alternatively, use ordinary dice with older children.

Further ideas
■ Use the photocopiable sheet 'Across the stones' on page 74 and play the game using the cube as a dice. Let the children see if they can roll the dice and move across the desert, using the stepping stones to get from one shelter to the other.
■ Play traditional board games such as 'Snakes and ladders'.

Buried treasure

What you need
Sand tray; dry sand; cardboard; gold foil; scissors; small lids of varying sizes; box with lid; sequins; beads; gold paint.

Preparation
Create a pirate's treasure chest by painting a box gold and gluing sequins and beads to the surface. Use the lids as templates and draw round them to create ten cardboard circles of varying sizes. Cut out the circles and cover them with gold foil to represent coins. Hide the coins under the sand in the sand tray.

What to do
Show the children the box and explain that it is a pirate's treasure chest but that the pirate lost his treasure when he landed on a desert island.

Invite the children to search for the buried treasure hidden in the sand and put it back into the chest.

Once the children are satisfied that they have found all of the treasure and returned it to the chest, invite them to tip the coins onto the carpet.

Ask the children to look at the coins. How many do they think there are? Invite them to take turns to count to check their guesses.

Suggest that the children close their eyes while you hide a different number of coins. Repeat the activity.

Leave time for the children to play the game together, taking turns to hide coins, find them, guess how many there are, and then check the guess by counting what they have found.

Support and extension
Hide up to five coins for younger children to find. Number ten coins and ask older children to arrange them in order after they have found them all.

Further ideas
■ Play variations of the game, for example, hiding ten numbered stones outdoors.
■ Invite the children to play with balance scales and small plastic bears. Suggest that they try to make the pans balance using bears of the same size. Count the bears. Are there the same number of bears in each pan? What happens if the same number of bears of a different size are put in one pan?

Marble runs

What you need
Sand tray; wet sand; cardboard tubes of different widths and lengths, such as carpet roll, kitchen roll and foil tubes; marbles; a small tea-tray.

What to do
Invite the children to choose a marble and roll it along a flat surface and then down a ramp created from a tea-tray.

Ask the children if they think their marbles will roll across wet sand as easily and then let them try to see what happens.

Invite the children to say how they think they could make their marbles roll more easily in the sand. Try out their suggestions, for example, building hills and slopes with their hands.

Ask whether the children think the cardboard tubes could be used to help the marbles to roll. They might suggest rolling marbles through them or using them to push marbles down the hills they have made.

Demonstrate how to press the tubes onto a sand slope and then lift them up again to create channels of different widths for the marbles to roll down. Have fun creating marble runs in this way.

As the children are playing, introduce appropriate mathematical language to describe the journeys of the marbles and the size of the channels, for example, talking about how the marbles roll from the top of a narrow slope down to the bottom using words such as 'top', 'middle', 'bottom', 'flat', 'slope', 'steep', 'long', 'wide' and 'narrow'.

Support and extension
Cut the tubes in half and lay them on slopes of sand so that younger children can roll their marbles down them easily. Encourage older children to make predictions, for example, whether the gradient of the slope will affect the speed the marbles roll at.

Further ideas
■ Bury tubes under the sand to create tunnels and roll the marbles through
■ Roll balls down more complex runs in a large outdoor sand-pit using carpet tubes or lengths of plastic piping and guttering.
■ Introduce the words 'sphere', 'cube' and 'cylinder' as you roll different objects such as ping-pong balls, wooden blocks and cardboard cylinders down slopes. Which shape rolls most successfully?

On balance

What you need
Sand tray; dry sand; small pebbles; a rocker scale; sand scoops; a short plank.

What to do
Put some dry sand in the sand tray and lay the plank across the centre, supported by two sides of the tray. Stand the rocker scale on the plank.

Talk about the rocker scale and the position of the two pans on each end. Are they at the same level? Invite one of the children to push a pan down with a finger and then to lift the finger off again. What happens?

Choose another child to put a small number of pebbles in one pan. What happens? Can the children say which pan is heaviest and which is lightest? Can they suggest ways of making the pans level again? Encourage the children to try out their suggestions and give lots of praise for their efforts.

Introduce appropriate language such as 'heavier', 'lighter', 'balance', 'more' and 'less' and encourage the children to use the words as they are working.

Suggest balancing the pans with pebbles in one and sand in the other. Is it easier to make the pans balance if pebbles are put in first or sand?

Allow lots of time for the children to explore freely and interact with questions to encourage them to use new vocabulary and express their ideas verbally.

Support and extension
Encourage younger children to play freely with the resources and talk them through their actions, using appropriate vocabulary but explaining this to make sure they understand your meaning. Suggest that older children choose other things to balance such as small-world characters and then invite them to represent their findings pictorially, for example, by drawing the scale with three people in one pan and three in the other pan.

Further ideas
■ Use scales to weigh ingredients when following recipes.
■ Use a large bucket balance outdoors to balance natural materials such as soil, small stones or leaves.

Brush and comb!

What you need
Sand tray; wet sand; tools to flatten and smooth the sand such as a carpet brush, sand rake and sand trowel; dowelling; fretsaw; vice; woodwork bench; PVA glue; thick card; large scissors.

Preparation
Create some sand combs with rectangles of thick card, approximately 20cms by 10cms. Cut lengths of dowelling, the same length as the card, using a fretsaw. Strengthen one of the long edges of the card by gluing a piece of dowelling along it. Cut triangles or arches along the opposite edge, some the same distance apart and others of varying distances.

What to do
Invite the children to think of ways to make the wet sand in the tray flat and smooth. Introduce the resources listed, and try out the children's ideas.

Demonstrate how to move the sand with the combs, and talk together about the pattern created.

Invite the children to create some straight lines the same distance apart. Which comb do they think they will use to do this? Now suggest creating wavy lines, still the same distance apart. Will the same comb work for this? Try using a comb that creates lines of varying distances from one another.

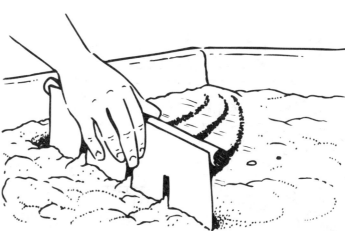

Play freely with the combs, talking about the lines being the 'same' distance, 'nearer' and 'further away' from each other.

Support and extension
Talk younger children through their actions as they explore the combs, using words such as 'line', 'straight', 'wavy' and 'pattern'. Invite older children to design their own combs, supporting them as they cut the wood and card.

Further ideas
■ Try using the combs to spread thick paint across a washable surface. Create swirling patterns and take prints of them by pressing a sheet of paper over the top and peeling it off.
■ Make symmetrical patterns using string. Dip a length of string in thick paint and arrange it in a pattern on one half of the paper, with a piece overlapping the end. Fold the paper over and hold it down while pulling the string out. Open out the paper to observe the design created. Display the children's creations in the classroom.

Ten tall penguins

What you need
Large bowl; water; blue food colouring; books with pictures of penguins; a copy of the song 'Ten tall penguins' on the photocopiable sheet on page 75; ten small-world penguins; waterproof marker.

Preparation
Write numerals from one to ten on the white chests of the penguins with a waterproof marker. After checking for allergies, add blue colouring to the water in the bowl.

What to do
Look at the books to find pictures of penguins. Talk about the environment in which they live.

Discuss how penguins move. Ask the children to pretend to be the tall penguins in the song, moving around with their arms close to their sides and stretching their bodies upwards.

Invite the children to sit in a circle on a washable floor with the bowl of coloured water in the centre representing a pool. Introduce the penguins and explain that you would like each child to 'look after' two of them, helping them to dive in the water and climb out again.

Sing the first verse of the song, pausing at the end to ask, 'Who has penguin number ten?'. The child with that penguin should help it to dive into the pool.

Once all the penguins are in the pool suggest that the children sing the song in reverse order until the penguins have jumped out again.

Support and extension
Adjust the words to the song so that there are just five penguins with younger children. Develop older children's number recognition skills by holding up number cards at random and inviting the children to make their penguins jump into the pool when the appropriate number is held up.

Further ideas
■ Invite the children to take the part of the penguins. Use a blue sheet cut into a circle to represent a pool. Make ten large bibs from the white sheeting and sew on black fabric numerals. Sing the song as the children dive into the pool one by one.
■ Write numbers on small-world creatures to make props for other water related number rhymes like 'Five Little Speckled Frogs' and 'Five Little Ducks'.

Noah's ark

What you need
Water tray; water; plastic margarine tub; card; sticky tape; glue; scissors; pairs of small-world animals; strip of wood; knowledge of the story of *Noah's Ark* by Heather Amery from *Usborne Bible Stories* (Usborne).

What to do
Tell the children the story of Noah's Ark and explain how this is a story from the bible.

Make an ark together from recycled materials. Choose an appropriate waterproof container, such as a margarine tub, to create the base. Make the roof from card.

Invite the children to sort through a selection of small-world animals to find five matching pairs. Arrange the pairs in two rows. Count one of the rows together and ask the children how many animals they think will be in the other row. Can they give a reason? Count the second row to check that it is the same.

Create a ramp from a strip of wood and invite the children to walk a pair of animals into the ark.

Continue to walk pairs of animals into the ark. Talk to the children about their actions, for example, 'There are two animals in the ark; let's add another two. How many are in the ark now?'

Put the ark in the water and see if it floats. If it is too heavy suggest taking two animals out.

Allocate the children free time to play with the ark.

Support and extension
Put five different animals in a line and ask younger children to find matching animals from a selection, saying, 'Here is a monkey. Can you find another one for me?' Present older children with practical problems involving addition and subtraction, for example, 'There are ten animals in the ark. If we take four out how many will be left?'.

Further ideas
■ Make two copies of the photocopiable sheet 'Into the Ark' on page 76 and suggest that the children cut out the animals and stick them to a large painting of an ark.
■ Re-enact the story of Noah's Ark with the children taking the part of the animals, wearing masks. Introduce simple problems associated with adding on and taking away.

How many more?

What you need
Water tray; water; food colouring; plastic bottles of varying sizes; plastic jugs and funnels; waterproof tape or marker pens; scissors; short plank.

Preparation
Lay the plank across the centre of the water tray to act as a stand. Colour the water with food colouring so that children can see it clearly. (Check for any allergies first.)

What to do
Show the children the bottles and talk about the different sizes. Which is the largest one? Which is the smallest?

Stand the largest bottle on the plank. Explain that you would like the children to fill it up using the smallest bottle. How many times do they think they will have to fill the small bottle and tip it into the large one before the large one is full? Discuss what the children have found out.

Demonstrate how a funnel helps to pour water directly into the bottle without any spillage. Suggest that the children take turns to fill the small bottle and pour it into the large one. Count as each bottle is tipped in. Is it easy to remember how many small bottles were needed?

Suggest marking the level of water in the large bottle with tape or a marker pen after the water from each small bottle is poured in so that the children can count the markings when the bottle is full.

Encourage the children to explore the bottles and other resources freely. Interact with appropriate language such as 'more' and 'less'. and make comparisons between the numbers of bottles required to fill different sized bottles.

Support and extension
Encourage younger children to play freely, filling and emptying bottles and talk to them as they do so, using appropriate vocabulary. Introduce graded measuring jugs, cylinders and funnels to extend the play of older children.

Further ideas
■ Invite children to pour out drinks for their friends at snack time, ensuring that they all have equal amounts.
■ Help the children to mix play dough, inviting them to count out how many cups or spoons of the ingredients are needed.

Sailing the high seas

What you need
Water tray; water; four ice-cream cartons; small-world people.

What to do
Provide each child with an ice-cream carton and explain that this represents a boat. Invite them to float their boats on the water tray.

Introduce the small-world people and ask the children to estimate how many people will fit into their boat before the boat is full, or capsizes. Write down each estimate.

Invite each child to choose a small-world character to put into their boat. Then suggest that they put in 'one more' and ask them, 'How many people are in the boat now? Is the boat full yet?'.

Continue to add people one at a time, asking questions and counting as you go, until the boat is too full or capsizes.

Talk about whether the boat would still float is there was 'one less' in it. Allocate time at the end of the activity for free exploration.

Support and extension
Encourage younger children to play freely with their boats and the characters, talking to them as they are playing, for example, saying 'You have put another person in your boat. There is still lots of room. Are you going to put someone else in?'. Invite older children to make up and write down stories about the characters they have created.

Further ideas
■ Play games involving fishing for plastic sea creatures with a net. Talk about how many are in the net and how many there would be if one jumped back out.

■ Invite the children to build towers with five blocks, either individually or in pairs and then ask them how many there would be if they added one more or took one away. Test their answers by counting.

■ Suggest that the children play traditional counting games, such as snakes and ladders and hopscotch.

LEARNING OBJECTIVES
STEPPING STONE
Say with confidence the number that is one more than a given number.

EARLY LEARNING GOAL
Find one more or one less than a number from 1 to ten.

GROUP SIZE
Four children.

HOME LINKS
Suggest that parents and carers play similar games with their children in the bath using toy animals and plastic tubs.

Ripples and waves

What you need
Paddling pool or water tray; water; smooth round pebbles; balls of varying sizes; plastic or wooden cubes.

Preparation
Set up the paddling pool or water tray outdoors and fill it with water. Never leave the pool unattended once it has water inside and always empty it as soon as the activity is finished.

What to do
Invite the children to observe the surface of the paddling pool, or the water tray. Is the water smooth or wavy?

Ask the children what they think will happen if you drop a round pebble into the water. Discuss the comments they make before asking them to observe your action.

Did the children hear the splash? Where is the pebble now? What does the water look like? Is it still smooth? Talk about the circular ripples created.

Show the children a cube and ask what they think will happen when that is dropped into the water. Will it make a splash? Will there be ripples? Will they be circular or square? Will the cube float or sink?

Wait for the water to become still before dropping the cube into it. Talk about the children's observations.

Invite the children to take turns to choose something to drop into the water, predicting beforehand what will happen.

Support and extension
Encourage younger children to drop sponge balls into the water and talk to them about what is happening. Ask them to drop the biggest ball into the water and then the smallest. Invite older children to arrange the pebbles and balls in order of size, and to use appropriate language to describe them.

Further ideas
■ Create two-dimensional shapes of different sizes from coloured card. Invite the children to sort them according to shape, colour or size.
■ Spread shaving foam over a washable surface and invite the children to draw shapes of different sizes in the foam with their fingers.

Knowledge and understanding of the world

This chapter suggests activities to enable children to investigate the world around them, asking questions and showing curiosity. They are encouraged to learn about their own cultures and beliefs and those of others, and begin to use technology.

Fun with holes

What you need
Dry sand; sand tray; a selection of containers with holes such as colanders, sieves, flour dredgers, slotted spoons and plants pots; clear plastic bottles of varying sizes; sand scoops.

What to do
Pass around the containers and talk about their uses with the children. Why do they need holes? How big are the holes? Are they all the same size?

Suggest that the children try to fill the containers with sand. Can they say what happens to the sand and why?

Talk about the appearance of the sand leaving the container, for example, larger holes will make the sand fall in thick lines whereas smaller holes will distribute it finely over a wide area.

Invite the children to observe sand as it is poured through the containers from a height and then closer to the sand tray.

Support and extension
Encourage younger children to explore freely and talk to them about their actions. Pierce holes at different levels in clear plastic bottles of varying sizes using a bradawl, and invite older children to explore how the sand flows through them.

Further ideas
■ Pour identical amounts of dry sand into different containers and invite the children to estimate which container they think the sand will pass through first. Can they say why? Discuss how the sand falls at different rates, depending on the size and number of holes in the container.

■ Look at some sand timers before making a timer with two clear plastic bottles. Half fill one bottle with sand and fasten a piece of plastic over the top with sticky tape. Pierce a hole in the plastic and then tape the other bottle to the top of it. Secure the bottles tightly together with sticky tape. See what the children can do before the sand runs from one bottle to the other, for example, build a tower or complete a simple puzzle.

Magnetic attraction

LEARNING OBJECTIVES

STEPPING STONE
Show curiosity, observe and manipulate objects.

EARLY LEARNING GOAL
Investigate objects and materials using all of their senses as appropriate.

GROUP SIZE
Up to six children.

What you need
Dry sand; a sand tray; metal objects, such as a toy car, paper clip and teaspoon; wooden objects, such as a pencil, building block and jigsaw piece; plastic objects, such as a peg, button and cup.

What to do
Arrange the objects on a table and encourage the children to explore them freely. Ask appropriate questions to encourage them to talk about their observations. Are the objects hard or soft, hot or cold, heavy or light?

Invite each child to name and describe a chosen object to the others.

Separate the objects into groups, sorted according to the material they are made from.

Suggest that the children hide the objects under the sand and see if they can find them again by moving a magnet over the surface.

Discuss why certain objects can be pulled from the sand with the magnet while others remain hidden. Do the objects attracted to the magnet have anything in common?

Support and extension
Hide only magnetic objects in the sand and encourage younger children to take turns to fish for them with a magnet. Invite older children to guess in advance whether an object is magnetic, and to explain the reason for this. Make a chart indicating objects that are attracted to magnets and those that are not.

Further ideas
■ Play a fishing game by attaching a small magnet to the end of some string tied to a stick. Cut out some paper fish and attach metal paper clips to the mouths of one half and plastic paper clips to the mouths of the other half. Invite the children to take turns to see who can catch the most fish in a given time. Talk about why some of the fish cannot be caught with the magnet and why others can.

■ Invite the children to explore the indoor and outdoor environment with magnets to discover which surfaces and objects are magnetic.

HOME LINKS
Ask the children to bring in magnetic objects from home for an interactive display.

Grand prix drivers

What you need
A copy of the photocopiable sheet 'Race track' on page 77; wet sand; a sand tray or outdoor sand-pit; toy racing cars; recycled materials, such as plastic plumbing pipes and small cardboard boxes; sand tools, such as spades, scoops, trowels and combs.

What to do
Show the children the toy cars and talk about their experience of racing cars. Have they ever seen races on television? Suggest making a sand race track.

Invite the children to flatten some wet sand in a sand tray, or outdoor sand-pit, using their hands and sand tools.

Use the racetrack on the photocopiable sheet to give the children ideas for the track layout. Work together to form the track by pressing a channel into the sand.

Talk about where the children might put additional features, such as a hill, tunnel and bridge, and how they could create them. Can they be made simply with sand?

Start by making a hill with moulded sand. Talk about the purpose of the hill. Will the moulded hill support the cars? Perhaps a cardboard box underneath would help to give more strength?

Try making a tunnel from sand. Will this be safe for the cars to travel through? Suggest using a plastic pipe to form a stronger tunnel and then cover it with sand.

Create a bridge from recycled boxes across the track.

Allow time for free play with the finished track.

Support and extension
Encourage younger children to help to make a simple track with short tunnels created from plastic plumbing pipes. Leave plenty of time for free play. Challenge older children by asking them to design written signs and flags to extend their play.

Further ideas
■ Take the children to a local bridge and walk over it. Discuss the shape and the materials used to construct it. Suggest that the children make model bridges from recycled materials or construction equipment.
■ Invite children to follow the track on the photocopiable sheet with a finger or pencil from 'Start' to 'Finish'.

LEARNING OBJECTIVES
STEPPING STONE
Investigate construction materials.

EARLY LEARNING GOAL
Select the tools and techniques they need to shape, assemble and join materials they are using.

GROUP SIZE
Up to eight children, depending on the size of the sand area.

HOME LINKS
Suggest that parents and carers talk to the children about the tools they use to clean and make repairs to things in the home.

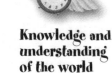

Miniature parks

What you need
Leaflets, pictures and photographs of local parks; wet sand; sand tray or washing-up bowl; plastic flowers; pebbles; twigs; moss; foil; blue ribbon; small-world play equipment such as swings, slides and climbing frames; small-world characters.

Preparation
Visit the tourist information office to obtain brochures and leaflets depicting local parks.

What to do
Look at the information about local parks, and ask the children about whether they have visited them. Discuss their memories of these and similar visits, and of specific events that they have enjoyed, such as playing hide-and-seek behind a tree or having a picnic.

Suggest that the children create a park using wet sand in the sand tray or washing up bowl, for small-world characters to enjoy.

Make paths in the sand from pebbles, add a piece of foil to represent a pond and a long piece of blue ribbon to represent a river.

Talk about what might be growing in the park and add resources, for example, plastic flowers, twigs for trees and moss for grass.

Discuss what the visiting children might like to play on and introduce the small-world swings, slide and climbing frame.

Encourage the children to play freely with the park, adding resources they think of as they do so, for example, putting model ducks on the pond.

Support and extension
Younger children will enjoy playing freely with the park after older children have helped staff to set it up. Talk to them as they play to encourage them to recall related past experiences. Encourage older children to talk about emotions associated with different occasions, stimulated by recollections of pleasurable memories of family outings. Discuss family celebrations and any cultural differences.

Further ideas
■ Make an interactive display entitled 'Happy memories' using the children's drawings paintings, photographs and appropriate objects.

LEARNING OBJECTIVES
STEPPING STONE
Remember and talk about significant things that have happened to them.

EARLY LEARNING GOAL
Find out about past and present events in their own lives, and those of their families and other people they know.

GROUP SIZE
Four children.

HOME LINKS
Invite parents and carers, friends or relatives from different cultures to talk to the children about their own happy memories from their past, including those associated with celebrations and festivals.

Life in the desert

What you need
Books about life in the desert; dry sand; sand tray; foil; appropriate small-world equipment, such as palm trees, camels, lizards, snakes and people; lollipop sticks; small fabric scraps; sticky tape; PVA glue.

What to do
Look at the books about life in the desert and make comparisons with the children's own lives. How do clothes, homes and foods differ?

Suggest that the children create a desert landscape in the sand tray by making drifts of sand and sand dunes with their hands.

Look again at the books about the nomadic way of life and construct small tents by attaching fabric scraps to lollipop sticks with tape or glue. Talk about similarities and differences between the children's houses and the tents that they have made.

Refer to the books for pictures of desert animal life and add model animals to the landscape. Talk about how animals survive in desert conditions.

Emphasise how living things need water in order to survive. Talk about where the supply of water comes from to our homes. Emphasise the lack of water in the desert and ask the children to imagine how they would manage with very little water. Make an oasis out of foil to add to the desert scene.

Support and extension
Set up the desert landscape as a free play activity for younger children and introduce appropriate new vocabulary as you interact with them. Use a map of the world to show older children where desert areas are located.

Further ideas
■ Construct other environmental landscapes using sand or soil as a base, such as a rain forest or jungle, or use salt to create an icy polar landscape.
■ Make a role-play tent using a brown blanket draped over a table or pop-up tent.
■ Investigate growth in different conditions with seeds planted in pots of sand and soil, for example, varying the amount of water and sunlight.

Go with the flow

What you need
A copy of the photocopiable sheet 'Pipe puzzle' on page 78; a selection of plastic plumbing pipes and connecting pieces; water tray; water; plastic jugs; plastic funnels; a short plank; electric drill; wide bit.

Preparation
Drill some holes in a short length of planking using a wide bit, so that a plastic pipe can be pushed through. Lay the plank across the centre of a water tray.

What to do
Show the children pipework leading to washbasins and sinks. Watch and listen as water travels down a pipe into a drain.

Introduce the selection of pipes and suggest that the children pretend to be plumbers connecting them together. Look at the pipe puzzle on the photocopiable sheet to stimulate the children's ideas.

Demonstrate how pipes can be made to stand securely in the holes in the plank before the children begin to play.

Talk about what happens when water is poured into the open ends of pipes. Invite the children to work in pairs to pour water into their pipework constructions. Suggest that one child pours water into the top of a pipe while the other holds it steady. Demonstrate how funnels help to direct the flow of water and make pouring easier, and let the children continue to experiment.

Can the children predict where the water will emerge? Were their predictions correct?

Support and extension
Invite younger children to stand pipes in the holes in the plank and put a funnel in the top of each one. Can they pour water into the funnel without spilling any? Encourage older children to design and make their own water pipe constructions, and suggest that they draw their finished designs.

Further ideas
■ Observe pipes attached to the sides of buildings. What are they made of? How are they connected? Talk about their function.
■ Set up marble runs using cardboard tubes cut in half and taped together. Does the gradient of the slopes affect the speed at which the marble rolls?
■ Complete the piping puzzle on the photocopiable sheet. Invite the children to guess where the water will come out if it is poured into each of the numbered pipes. Let them check with their fingers and write in the numbers in the boxes.

Chilly investigations

What you need
Containers suitable for creating different shapes with ice, such as a cup, jelly mould and plastic chocolate box tray; an ice-cube tray; water; food colouring; plastic jugs; a plastic tray; a fridge with a frozen food compartment or a freezer.

Preparation
Prepare some ice cubes. Check for food allergies and intolerances.

What to do
Talk to the children about their experiences of using a fridge and freezer.

Tip a tray of ice cubes onto a plastic tray, and talk about their size and shape. (Emphasise that the children should not touch ice taken straight from the freezer.)

Suggest using the freezer to make ice of different sizes, colours and shapes using the moulds.

Ask the children to choose a colour for the ice. Add drops of their chosen food colour, or colours, to some water in a jug and invite the children to choose a mould to fill.

Transfer the moulds to a plastic tray and put the tray into the freezer.

Visit the freezer regularly to see if the moulds are frozen. Compare the time taken for different moulds to freeze and discuss the reasons why.

Once frozen remove the moulds from the freezer. What changes have occurred?

Empty the frozen shapes onto a plastic tray. Can the children identify their chosen shape?

Watch the ice moulds melt and encourage the children to discuss their observations.

Support and extension
Suggest that younger children are supported by their younger friends as they pour the coloured water into the moulds. Ask older children to consider what colour the resulting liquid will be if ice cubes of two different colours were melted in the same bowl. Test their ideas.

Further ideas
■ Visit a freezer shop, or frozen food department in a supermarket, to buy something frozen. Discuss how freezers work and make comparisons with the freezers in the children's homes.
■ Fill three identical bowls with water and put one on a windowsill, one in the fridge and one in the freezer. Allow the water in the freezer to freeze before making comparisons between the contents of the bowls.

Water music

What you need
Battery-operated cassette player; cassettes of music representing water, for example, Handel's *Water music* or *La Mer* by Debussy; water tray; warm water; washing-up liquid; blue food colouring; towels.

Preparation
Prepare the contents of the water tray to stimulate soothing, relaxing exploration by adding warm water, food colouring and washing-up liquid. Swish the water around to create bubbles. Check for allergies to any of the resources used.

What to do
Invite the children to sit in a comfortable position on a carpet to listen to the examples of music on a battery-operated cassette recorder. Suggest that they close their eyes and imagine a river, stream or big ocean. Explain that the composers thought that their music sounded like flowing water. Do the children agree?

Together, choose one of the pieces of music to listen to while the children play with the water. Show the children how to insert the cassette into the recorder and to operate the controls. Stress the importance of having dry hands, and ensure that the recorder is a good distance away from the water tray to protect it from damage.

Encourage the children to listen to the music while moving their hands in the water. Emphasise the importance of playing quietly so that others can enjoy the music.

If the music contains water sounds, ask the children to try and mimic the sounds they can hear using the water in the tray.

Support and extension
Put the music on for younger children, but encourage them to watch as you operate the cassette recorder. Talk about your actions. Invite older children to choose their own music and operate the cassette recorder themselves.

Further ideas
■ Record your own version of water music. Invite some children to play percussion instruments while others pour, trickle and splash water noises in the background.
■ Dance and move freely to the water music used in this activity, encouraging children to operate the cassette recorder with supervision.

Moving along

What you need
A selection of small plastic boats; drinking straws; small battery-operated fans; thick paper; sticky tape.

Preparation
Plan a session beforehand for the children to make boats from recycled materials such as margarine tubs and clean plastic meat trays.

What to do
Talk about windy weather and ask the children to recall walking on a very windy day. How did they feel? Discuss the effects of the wind, for example, leaves falling off trees or washing blowing on a line.

Invite the children to float plastic and homemade boats in the water tray. Can they think of ways to make the boats move without touching them?

Suggest making paper fans by folding a rectangle of thick paper backwards and forwards. Gather up the folds along one side and tape them securely together to form a handle. Demonstrate how to wave the fans to create a draught. Do they move the boats effectively?

Encourage the children to consider other ways of creating a breeze, such as blowing through a straw or using their mouths, and test out these ideas.

Support and extension
Younger children will enjoy simply floating boats on the water and blowing them along with straws. Show older children how to operate small hand held battery-operated fans and suggest that they use them to move their boats. Emphasise that they should never touch electric fans.

Further ideas
■ Show the children how to create paint patterns by dropping a large blob of paint onto a sheet of paper and blowing it along using a drinking straw. Ensure that the children are mature enough to manage this activity as young children might suck the paint into their mouths.
■ Make homemade flags or kites with the children using fabric attached to sticks. Take them outdoors on a windy day to see how they fly in the wind.
■ Make and decorate paper boats. Hold water tray boat races to celebrate the Chinese Dragon Boat Festival, using different methods of creating wind, such as paper fans, electric fans, straws, or blowing.

Scrub and scrape

What you need
Water tray; water; a selection of vegetables from around the world, such as sweet potato, aubergine and courgette; scrubbing brushes; plastic pan scrubs; plastic toy pans; bowls; spoons; ladles; colanders.

Preparation
Encourage parents and carers to provide vegetables from their country of origin, or purchase a selection if there is little cultural diversity within your group.

What to do
Put some water into a water tray until it is deep enough to cover the selection of vegetables. Encourage the children to play freely with the vegetables along with the additional resources described above.

Spend time with the children pretending to cook and serve imaginary meals with the vegetables, talking about their texture, smell, size, colour and shape as you do so. Let the children play freely.

Invite the children to name the vegetables that they know and tell them the names of the more unusual examples.

Support and extension
Put just two contrasting vegetables into the water, one familiar and one from another culture, for younger children to explore. After playing, encourage older children to remove the vegetables from the water and talk about their countries of origin.

Further ideas
■ Make a soup from the vegetables used. Provide each child with a chopping board, peeler and kitchen knife and suggest that they chop up small pieces of the vegetables and put them in a large pan. Add a stock cube and boil the vegetables away from the children. Allow the soup to cool before inviting the children to sample it.
■ Make prints with the children by dipping cross-sections of vegetables into coloured paint and then onto paper.
■ Create an interactive display to show the country of origin of different vegetables on a map of the world. Ask the children to cut out pictures of different vegetables from magazines to attach to the wall display. Arrange samples of vegetables on a table below and join them to their countries of origin with lengths of string.

Physical development

These ideas encourage children to move within a space with confidence, control, coordination and safety, as well as to recognise the importance of keeping healthy. They will learn to handle tools, objects and other materials with an increasing degree of control.

Busy builders

What you need
Books about house building; photographs of builders at work; plans of buildings; wheelbarrows; plastic bricks; spades; sand trowels; buckets; hard hats; Wellington boots; reflective jackets; an outside sand-pit; sand; clipboards; pencils; storage containers; water; watering cans.

Preparation
Take photographs of builders at work mixing cement, laying bricks and transporting materials in wheelbarrows. Put the writing tools and materials, and the hats and jackets, in two separate containers.

What to do
Before going outside, look at the books and photographs together and talk about the children's experiences of observing builders at work.

Go outside to the sand-pit and show the children the hard hats, boots and reflective jackets. Talk about why this special clothing is necessary on a building site.

Look at the resources for transporting and moulding sand and discuss how walls are created from bricks and mortar. Suggest that the children mix sand and water together to form 'pretend' cement to stick plastic bricks together. Show the children some building plans and suggest that they draw plans of the buildings they plan to create on the paper, attached to the clipboards.

Allow plenty of free time for the children to explore the resources and develop their ideas.

Support and extension
Encourage younger children to move confidently among others as they play freely in the sand. Suggest that older children work in pairs, taking turns to dig the sand and put it in a wheelbarrow, and to hold the barrow steady.

Further ideas
■ Suggest moving the building site to another area within the outdoor space. Use wheelbarrows to transport the sand and trolleys to transport the bricks.
■ Visit a building site to observe builders at work. Ensure that children are closely supervised at all times.
■ Invite a builder, or students from a technical local college, to demonstrate their work.

Skilful fingers

What you need
Washing-up bowl; dry sand; sand scoops; a selection of small objects such as paper clips, coins, pegs, beads, fabric scraps and buttons; four small bowls; tweezers; sugar tongs; clothes pegs; four small shallow trays; sand timers.

What to do
Supply each child with a small tray and bowl.

Invite the children to cover the surface of their trays with a thick layer of dry sand, taken from a washing-up bowl.

Explore the selection of small objects together and ask the children to choose five things to put in their trays and cover these with their sand.

Demonstrate how the egg timer works and explain that you would like the children to see how many of the objects in their trays they can pick up and transfer to a bowl before the sand runs out.

Suggest that the children try picking up the objects with their fingers first before trying again, this time using one of the tools.

Allow time for the children to try out the different tools.

Talk about which objects were easiest to pick up and which were more difficult. Were some of the objects harder to pick up and did some tools work more efficiently?

Support and extension
Invite younger children to try picking up the objects without tools, and without the restrictions of the timer. Provide greater challenges to older children by increasing the number of objects to be picked up in a given time.

Further ideas
■ Provide the children with 'post it' games involving fitting plastic shapes into matching holes, or create your own games by making cardboard lids for bowls with different shaped holes cut out of them. Invite the children to post the objects they pick up through the holes.
■ Play 'Find the short straw': stand some straws into dry sand, including one short one. Push them down until they look the same length. Ask the children to take turns to pull out a straw with a finger and thumb until one of them pulls out the short straw.

LEARNING OBJECTIVES
STEPPING STONE
Manipulate materials and objects by picking up, releasing, arranging, threading and posting them.

EARLY LEARNING GOAL
Move with control and coordination.

GROUP SIZE
Up to four children.

HOME LINKS
Suggest that parents and carers develop their children's manipulative skills by making necklaces with pasta tubes or buttons threaded onto string.

Quoit pits

What you need
Outdoor sand-pit; wet sand; plastic plumbing pipes; quoits or rubber rings; plastic cone.

Preparation
Cut the plastic pipes into short lengths.
Stand a cone at the opposite end of the play area, away from the sand-pit.

What to do
Stand the plastic pipes upright in the sand.
Invite the children to choose a quoit or rubber ring, and to take turns to throw it into the sand-pit with the aim of hitting a pipe.
When a child is successful in hitting a pipe, suggest that all the children run across the play area and around the back of the cone, before returning to continue the game.
How do the children feel after running? Do they feel out of breath? Do their cheeks feel warm?
Discuss why the heart beats faster during exercise. Invite each child to put a hand over a friend's heart. Can they feel it beating?
Talk about the importance of warming up before exercise and cooling down afterwards. Encourage the children to stretch their arms and legs before and after playing the game.

Support and extension
Simplify the game for younger children by inviting them to throw their rings into pits dug in the sand, and to run round the cone after each throw. Challenge older children to try to throw the quoit over a pipe rather than just hit it.

Further ideas
■ Invite the children to take turns to jump into the sand-pit. Suggest that they run up to the sand and then jump as far as they can. Ask the children to describe how their bodies feel after this exercise. Can they feel their leg muscles stretching?
■ Set up an obstacle course with activities involving small apparatus at points along a circuit, for example, throwing a beanbag into a bucket or balancing along a rope. Which activity is the most tiring?

Sand mousse

What you need
Small sand tray; large bucket filled with water; dry sand; hand and balloon whisks; tablespoon; jug; sand tools, such as scoops, rakes, spades and buckets.

What to do
Fill the bottom of the sand tray with water to a depth of approximately 2cm.

Provide the children with a large bucket of dry sand and invite them to fill a jug with sand from the bucket and add it to the water.

Suggest that they whisk the sand into the water until it is fully mixed before adding another jug of sand.

Continue to add sand and whisk it until a thick mousse is formed. Invite the children to describe the appearance of the mousse. Can they see bubbles?

Talk about the difference between a hand whisk, operated by turning a handle, and a balloon whisk. How does the hand whisk work? Talk about 'pushing' the handle round and round. Observe how the cogs move when the handle is turned.

Continue to add sand until the mixture is too thick to whisk and then encourage the children to play freely using a range of sand tools.

Support and extension
Mix the sand and water in advance for younger children, show them how to use balloon whisks, and offer to help them if necessary. Suggest that older children mix milkshakes using clean whisks and then pour them into cups to serve to their friends.

Further ideas
■ Play a guessing game with actions. Stick pictures of household machines such as an iron, toaster, vacuum cleaner or hair dryer onto card. Invite each child to take a card and mime the movements associated with operating the pictured machine to the rest of the group. Encourage the others to guess the name of the machine from the mime they observe.

■ Make comparisons between hand-operated and electric whisks. Create a milk whip drink from a packet mix, using an electric mixer, while the children watch at a safe distance. Discuss what flavours the children enjoy, then invite them to wear aprons and suggest that they make a milk drink using a hand whisk.

Sparkle and shimmer

What you need
Dry sand; shallow cardboard trays such as shoe-box lids; shallow dishes; salt; glitter; salt shakers.

Preparation
Put the different coloured glitter into shallow dishes and fill up the shakers with salt.

What to do
Provide each child with a tray containing some dry sand and invite them to experiment with mixing salt and glitter into the sand to make it shine and sparkle. Encourage them to try adding different quantities of salt using the shakers and to sprinkle on the glitter with their fingers.

Ask the children to try sprinkling or shaking from different heights over the sand and to notice what difference this makes when the glitter or salt lands. Is it confined to a small area or spread across the entire surface?

Ask the children to pick up the trays with care and shake them gently from side to side so that the lighter glitter rises to the surface. Encourage the children to describe any changes they observe in the appearance of the mixture.

Support and extension
Add glitter to dry sand in a sand tray and invite younger children to explore it freely using a range of tools, such as scoops, rakes and wheels. Invite older children to create a shiny mixture in a sand tray by adding glitter to dry sand and then challenge them to direct the flow of the resulting mixture by introducing resources such as plastic tubing, pipes and funnels.

Further ideas
■ Invite the children to spread glue over some card before sprinkling their shiny sand mixture over it to make a sparkly picture. Leave the pictures to dry before mounting them to display beside the sand area.
■ Create a papier mâché landscape and invite the children to cover it with glue before sprinkling on their shiny mixtures. Use the resulting landscape for small-world seaside or dinosaur play.
■ Add glitter to glue and paint so that the children can create sparkling pictures or textured collage work.

Blowing bubbles

What you need
Water tray; water; washing-up liquid; drinking straws; narrow bore plastic plumbing pipes; flexible transparent plastic tubing; large bucket.

Preparation
Cut the pipes and tubing into suitable lengths so that the children can hold them securely as they blow down them.

Stand the pipes, tubes and straws in separate containers to encourage the children to make choices.

What to do
Invite the children to squeeze some washing-up liquid into the water and swish it around.

Show the children the selection of straws, pipes and tubes and demonstrate how to blow air through them into the soapy water. Emphasise the importance of blowing rather than sucking. Explain that the children should not share the resources for this activity, as this is how germs can be spread.

Encourage the children to play freely with the resources, trying to blow bubbles with straws, pipes and tubes, and putting them in a bucket after use to be washed later. Talk about the bubbles. Are they different sizes or all the same? Are they the same shape?

Invite the children to think about other things are spherical and to name them.

Invite the children to try blowing bubbles in a bowl of clear water without adding washing-up liquid. Were they successful?

Support and extension
Encourage younger children to blow through pipes into clear water until they have mastered the skill of blowing rather than sucking. Supply plastic wands for older children to use to blow bubbles outdoors.

Further ideas
■ Mix washing-up liquid into some watery paint in a circular margarine tub and invite the children to blow bubbles in the mixture until they rise above the rim of the tub. Show them how to press a sheet of paper lightly onto the bubbles and then lift it up again to reveal bubble prints underneath.

■ Encourage the children to create giant bubble wands by bending coat hangers into different shapes. Put a mixture of washing-up liquid and water into a shallow tray and dip the wand into it. Run holding the wand in the air to create elongated bubbles.

Invisible paint

What you need
Water; small buckets; decorator's brushes of different sizes; aprons; adult-sized white shirts; white caps; baby bath.

Preparation
Create overalls for the children by cutting down some adult-sized white shirts.

What to do
Talk to the children about the work of a painter. Have they ever seen a painter at work, or watched a member of the family painting the house?

Suggest that the children pretend to be painters, painting the fences or walls outdoors.

Discuss what painters wear. Why do they cover their clothes and hair? Invite the children to choose appropriate protective clothing from a selection of aprons, overalls and caps.

Look for suitable outdoor surfaces to paint. Provide the children with a selection of buckets and brushes, and a baby bath half-filled with water.

Encourage the children to 'paint' freely, supervising them closely as they fill their buckets from the baby bath. Replenish the water supply as often as necessary.

Return to the 'painted' surfaces at intervals and discuss what is happening as the water dries and eventually disappears.

Support and extension
Provide waterproof aprons and Wellingtons for younger children and encourage them to make large marks with very big brushes. Suggest that older children try to paint their names onto a wall or paving stone.

LEARNING OBJECTIVES
STEPPING STONE
Show a clear and consistent preference for the left or right hand.

EARLY LEARNING GOAL
Show an awareness of space, of themselves and of others.

GROUP SIZE
Up to six children.

Further ideas
■ Unroll a length of wallpaper along the ground outdoors and supply the children with thick crayons. Invite them to take a crayon for a 'straight line walk' and a 'wavy line walk' along the paper. Suggest that these lines become tracks to push small-world vehicles along.

■ On a dry day, create a puddle on a hard surface using a watering can. Draw round the edge of the puddle with thick white chalk and visit it at intervals to mark the edge with chalk as it evaporates. See how long it takes for the puddle to disappear. Does the puddle dry more quickly in certain weather conditions, for example, on a windy day or in hot sunshine?

HOME LINKS
Explain the activity to parents and carers so that they can encourage their children to pretend to be decorators 'painting' the outside of their houses.

Healthy living

What you need

Soap; water; paper towels; sink; bananas; apples; four chopping boards; four kitchen knives; two large bowls; lemon juice.

What to do

Explain to the children that you would like them to help you to prepare a fruit snack for the rest of the children.

Talk about the importance of washing hands before handling food and take the children through the process step-by-step. Observe them closely to ensure that they use resources effectively, washing your own hands to reinforce this importance.

Ask the children to help to wash the apples and dry them with paper towels.

Cut the apples into manageable-sized pieces and remove the pips before inviting the children to cut the pieces into slices and put them into a large bowl. Cover the apple with water and add a squeeze of lemon juice, explain to the children that this will stop the apples from turning brown.

Once the apples have been prepared invite the children to peel the bananas and slice them into another large bowl.

Suggest that the children wash their hands again before handing out the fruit to the rest of the children at snack time.

While the children are enjoying their snack reinforce the practices associated with cleanliness when handling food.

Support and extension

Encourage older children to be role models, demonstrating to younger children how to wash and dry their hands properly. Present younger children with a more manageable task such as slicing the bananas, and challenge older children, for example, by asking them to prepare apple slices of equal sizes. Involve the older children in washing the utensils and putting them away.

Further ideas

■ Invite children to scrub and chop vegetables to make soup.
■ Involve children in illustrating posters to be laminated and displayed in the washroom area to remind them about washing their hands after they have been to the toilet.
■ Keep a hand-washing chart linked to the children's daily routines to reinforce the message of cleanliness.

Make a splash

What you need
Small paddling pool; water; small balls; large balls; four hoops; bats; quoits.

Preparation
Blow up the paddling pool in a clear outdoor space and fill it with water. (Never leave the pool unattended once it has water inside and always empty it as soon as the activity has finished.)

What to do
Arrange the hoops around the paddling pool at a short distance from the edge.

Ask the children if they would like to play a game and explain that the object of the game is to stand in a hoop and throw a ball or quoit into the pool to create a big splash.

Have fun making splashes initially by simply throwing balls and quoits, before introducing the challenge of using bats to hit the balls.

Talk about the resources used. Do large balls make a bigger splash than small balls? Is it harder to manage to get a ball into the pool using a bat?

Support and extension
Put the hoops nearer to the pool so that younger children can manage more easily. Challenge older children by asking them to throw balls from a greater distance, or into buckets rather than a pool.

LEARNING OBJECTIVES
STEPPING STONE
Use increasing control over an object by touching, pushing, patting, throwing, catching or kicking it.

EARLY LEARNING GOAL
Use a range of small and large equipment.

GROUP SIZE
Four children.

Further ideas
■ Fill plastic bottles with water and create an outdoor bowling alley. Invite the children to take turns to bowl a large ball at the bottles and count how many are knocked down each time.
■ Tie curtain rings to the heads of plastic ducks before floating them in a paddling pool. Invite the children to catch the ducks using home-made fishing rods. Create the rods by tying a length of string to the end of a garden cane and attaching a hook to the end of the string.
■ Play beanbag 'hopscotch': arrange the hoops in a row and invite the children to take turns to stand at one end and try to throw a beanbag into each hoop, starting with the nearest one. After each throw, retrieve the beanbag by jumping from hoop to hoop.

HOME LINKS
Encourage parents and carers to play traditional games with their children involving aiming at a target, for example, football or tiddly-winks.

Sink or float?

What you need
Clay; four small margarine tubs; water; water tray.

What to do
Provide the children with some clay to play with freely before suggesting that they create balls by rolling the clay in the palms of their hands. Encourage them to try and make the balls approximately the same size.

Invite the children to put one of their clay balls onto the water. What happens to it?

Show the children the margarine tubs and invite them to choose one to put onto the water. Does it float or sink?

Suggest that the children try putting a clay ball into the tub. What happens? Ask them to continue adding the balls one by one until the tub sinks, counting them as they do so. How many balls does it take to sink the tub?

Suggest making balls of different sizes. Is it possible to make one ball large enough to sink the tub?

Encourage the children to play freely with the resources and talk about their observations.

What happens to clay after it sinks? Stir the balls around until they disintegrate. What colour is the water now?

Support and extension
Encourage younger children to play freely with the clay to become familiar with how it feels and behaves. Show older children how to transform their clay balls into small bowls by pushing a thumb into the centre and pressing outwards in a circle. What happens when the bowls are put gently onto the surface of the water? Do they float or sink?

Further ideas
■ Invite the children to make boats from Plasticine for small-world people to sail across the water tray. How many can travel in the boat before it sinks?
■ Mix clay with water to create mud. Invite the children to wear aprons and have fun making mud pies.

Creative development

This chapter suggests a wide range of ideas to help children explore sound and music, as well as beginning to look at shape, form and texture in two or three dimensions and using their imaginations in stories, music, art and design, dance and role-play.

Sand artists

What you need
Dry sand; powder paint; small bowls; teaspoons; card; PVA glue; glue spreaders.

What to do
Explain to the children that you are going to show them how to create some coloured pictures using sand.

Ask the children to help to fill several small bowls with dry sand and to take turns to choose a different coloured powder paint.

Pass around the bowls and invite each child to add a few teaspoons of their chosen powder paint to the sand in the bowl and to mix it up well. Talk about the changes in the appearance of the sand as the children mix in the paint.

Put the bowls of coloured sand back into the centre of the table so that all of the children can reach them.

Supply the children with a sheet of white card each and suggest that they cover the surface with a layer of PVA glue.

Demonstrate how to sprinkle the sand carefully onto the glue, before suggesting that the children add different coloured sands to the glue to create patterns and shapes. What happens when they sprinkle different sands on top of one another?

Dry the pictures thoroughly and then invite the children to feel the texture of their creations.

Allow time for the children to make several pictures so that they can explore the effects of mixing colours.

Support and extension
Put the coloured sand into flour shakers so that younger children can apply it more easily. Encourage older children to form 'feely' numbers and letters by covering card outlines with glue and sprinkling sand onto them.

Further idea
■ Supply the children with pre-cut card shapes so that they can create coloured sandpaper triangles, circles, squares and rectangles.
■ Cut out gingerbread men shapes for the children to coat with dry coloured sand and display their creations.

Shake to the beat

What you need
Grit; coarse sand; fine sand; small bowls; identical clear plastic bottles with screw tops; coloured tape; funnels; pair of maracas.

Preparation
Attach strips of different coloured tape at regular intervals, and in the same sequence, around each bottle.

Put the grit, fine sand and coarse sand into different bowls.

What to do
Show the maracas to the children and pass them around to listen to the sound they make. Explain that you would like the children to help you to make some maracas from plastic bottles.

Pass around bowls of grit, coarse sand and fine sand so that the children can feel the differences in the textures.

Demonstrate how to put a funnel into the neck of a bottle and pour sand through it up to the level of the first strip of tape. Invite the children to do the same, adding their own choice of filling to the bottles.

Screw the tops on the bottles and listen to the sound they make as the children shake them one by one. Is there a difference in the sound? Which filling creates the loudest or softest sound?

Fill a bottle with sand up to the second tape marker. Compare the sound made by this bottle with the sound made by a bottle filled to the first marker. Is there any difference?

Continue to explore the sounds created using different types and quantities of filling.

Support and extension
Make the shakers beforehand for younger children and concentrate on comparing the sounds they make. Encourage older children to copy rhythms created by adults shaking maracas.

Further ideas
■ Create maracas from washing-up liquid bottles with lengths of dowelling pushed into the lids to create handles. Varnish the surface with a mixture of paint and PVA glue and decorate with stick-on sequins.
■ Make sandpaper blocks from wood offcuts covered in sandpaper. Invite the children to rub them together in time to some music.
■ Accompany the song 'Down by the sea' on the photocopiable sheet on page 79 with home-made shakers, maracas and sand blocks.

Sifting sounds

What you need
A copy of the photocopiable sheet 'Find the instruments' on page 80; dry sand; sand tray; funnels; sieves; flour shaker; sound making resources such as metal pan lids, wooden and plastic chopping boards and newspaper; foil; box of percussion instruments.

What to do
Pass around the copy of the photocopiable sheet and invite the children to take turns to point to a musical instrument. Do they know the name of the instrument? Have they ever heard anyone play an instrument?

Explore a box of percussion instruments and ask the children to take turns to choose one to play. Talk about how the sounds differ.

Look at the selection of sound-making resources, such as metal lids, chopping boards and newspaper, and choose something to put in the bottom of an empty sand tray.

Sprinkle dry sand onto the bottom of the tray and then onto the chosen object. Does the sound change? Is it louder or quieter?

Encourage the children to explore the resources fully, sprinkling sand onto different surfaces with their fingers, and pouring it through sieves, flour shakers and funnels. Talk about what the sounds remind them of, perhaps falling rain or wind, scattering leaves.

Support and extension
Encourage younger children to explore two contrasting sounds, for example, shaking dry sand through a sieve onto paper and then through a funnel onto a metal lid. Invite older children to explore ways of dampening sound, for example, by putting a layer of towelling over the surface of a pan lid or covering a drumstick in wool.

Further ideas
■ Make rainmakers by putting dry sand and grains of rice into a long cardboard tube and sealing the ends. Slowly turn the tube upside down to create the sound of rain.
■ Ask a musician to demonstrate how sound can be changed, for example, using loud and soft pedals on a piano or a mute on a trumpet.
■ Record the sounds made at the sand tray using a cassette recorder, and then make them louder or quieter using the volume control.

LEARNING OBJECTIVES
STEPPING STONE
Explore and learn how sounds can be changed.

EARLY LEARNING GOAL
Recognise and explore how sounds can be changed.

GROUP SIZE
Four children

HOME LINKS
Encourage parents and carers to help their children to create sounds at home using everyday items, such as pans and spoons, and then to try to dampen the sounds using different materials.

Sand sculptures

What you need
Sand; water; four play dough boards; icing bags or strong plastic food bags; sand scoops; bowl; photographs or pictures of worm casts.

Preparation
Take some photographs of worm casts in soil or on the beach. If icing bags are not available cut a hole in one corner of each food bag.

What to do
Invite the children to help you to create a thick mixture of sand and water in a bowl.

Demonstrate how to fill a bag with the mixture and squeeze it so that the sand comes through the hole like a long 'worm' onto a board.

Supply each child with a board and a bag. Have fun filling the bags and squeezing swirls and whirls of sand onto the boards. Encourage the children to talk about what they see, hear and feel as they play.

Look at the photographs or pictures of worm casts on sand. Have the children ever noticed them at the seaside or in the garden? Discuss their shape and introduce vocabulary such as 'swirl', 'twirl', 'twist' and 'turn'.

Support and extension
Demonstrate to younger children how to mould a sand shape in the sand tray before inviting them to try for themselves using buckets, moulds and wet sand. Cut holes of different sizes in the bags so that older children can make observations about the varying shapes and sizes of the sand tubes they create.

Further ideas
■ Demonstrate, by example, how to find collage materials needed when working creatively, and how to clear up afterwards, so that children are able to do this spontaneously when working by themselves.

■ Try squeezing play dough through the bags, a potato masher or a garlic press to create three-dimensional sculptures.

■ Demonstrate other creative techniques for children to imitate, for example, creating splatters, swirls or drips with paint brushes, or transforming a hand print into a tree by adding fingerprint 'fruit' and 'leaves'.

■ Make comparisons between icing bags and hand-held icing machines as you ice biscuits together.

Seaside holidays

What you need

A copy of the song 'Down by the sea' on the photocopiable sheet on page 79; sand tray; wet sand; small-world characters and sea creatures; scraps of towelling and fabric; cocktail sticks and umbrellas with the sharp ends removed; scraps of coloured paper; scissors; ice-cream tub spoons; thimbles; shells; small stones; shallow bowl; boats; water.

What to do

Sing the song 'Down by the sea' on the photocopiable sheet and invite the children to make up their own actions and verses.

Talk about the children's experiences of the seaside and suggest making a seaside for the small-world characters.

Put wet sand into a sand tray leaving a space in one corner for a shallow bowl. Put some water in the bowl to represent the sea and add some plastic sea creatures, stones and shells.

Encourage the children to create a seaside atmosphere by adding shells and small stones to the sand and by making their own props. For example, create towels from scraps of towelling, parasols from cocktail umbrellas, and flags from cocktail sticks and paper. Use thimbles for buckets and the ice-cream spoons as spades.

Allow lots of time for the children to play with the small-world characters at their 'seaside'.

Support and extension

Set up the seaside beforehand so that younger children can enjoy playing with the resources. Encourage older children to create their own stories about the small-world characters and to make suggestions for props.

Further ideas

■ Set up a role-play beach on a clear carpet area, using a yellow sheet to represent the beach and a folded blue one to represent waves on the sea. Drape a clothes horse in a striped sheet to form a windbreak. Spread resources such as shells, towels, buckets and spades in the area. Re-enact the song 'Down by the sea' in the area.

■ Create an outdoor seaside in the sand-pit with a role-play ice-cream kiosk and Punch and Judy show alongside. On hot days, include a paddling pool sea. (Ensure close supervision at all times.)

LEARNING OBJECTIVES
STEPPING STONE
Use available resources to create props to support role play.

EARLY LEARNING GOAL
Use their imagination in imaginative and role play and stories.

GROUP SIZE
Four children.

HOME LINKS
Suggest that parents and carers encourage their children to put on swimwear at bathtime and pretend to be fishing in the sea, catching model sea creatures in a plastic sieve.

Magic patterns

What you need
Marbling inks in different colours; droppers; a deep plastic tray; water; paper;
aprons.

What to do
Invite the children to put on aprons and explain that you are going to show
them a special way of painting to create 'magic patterns'.
    Put the tray in the centre of the table and fill it with water.
    Demonstrate how to fill the dropper by lowering it carefully into a bottle,
squeezing the nozzle and then releasing it carefully so that the ink is drawn
up into the tube.
    Put a few drops of the ink onto the surface of the water by gently squeezing
the nozzle of the dropper. Do this with another colour and talk to the children
about their observations as the two different colours spread across the surface
of the water.
    Lower a piece of paper onto the surface, making sure all of it is in contact
with the water. Lift the paper back up again very gently, holding it by one
corner, before turning the paper over to
reveal the pattern. Leave it to dry on a flat
surface.
    Encourage each child to try making a
pattern before adding more colour.
Allow lots of time to try different colour
combinations.

Support and extension
Substitute a mixture of cooking oil and
powder paint for marbling ink with younger
children and apply the mixture from an
empty washing-up liquid bottle. Encourage
older children to try putting cooking oil in
the tray and dropping a thin mixture of
powder paint and water onto the surface.
Comment on how the paper changes
appearance as the oil soaks into it.

Further ideas
■ Invite the children to use marbling prints to form mounts and frames for art
work and photographs.
■ Create the effect of waves on the sea by using shades of blue paint for
marbling. Dry the picture before adding sea creatures made from collage
materials.
■ Try other techniques requiring colour choices, for example, wax resist
pictures created by painting a watery wash of different colours over patterns
drawn with candles, or spatter paintings, made by flicking paint onto a black
background using an old toothbrush.

Colour merge

What you need
Three clear plastic bottles; funnels; jugs; food colourings; eye droppers; water; water tray; white insulating tape.

Preparation
Check for allergies to food colourings. Attach white insulating tape around each bottle, approximately a quarter of the distance from base to lid. Put a drop of red, blue or yellow food colouring into the bottom of each bottle so that each one contains a different colour. Half-fill the water tray with water.

What to do
Demonstrate how to use a funnel to fill a bottle and then invite the children to choose a bottle each and ask them to pour water into it so it reaches the level of the tape.

What colour is the water in the bottle? Can the children suggest why each one is different?

Show the children the bottles of food colourings and explain what they are used for. Add an extra drop of the appropriate colour to each bottle and watch as the colour deepens.

Choose two of the bottles and ask the children what they think will happen if they are poured into the water tray, one at each end. As you pour in the coloured water, watch as the colours gradually merge to make new colours and shades.

Support and extension
Colour the water in the tray in either red, blue or yellow and allow time for younger children to play, filling and emptying containers, before gradually pouring in another primary colour. Talk about the colour changes as they happen. Encourage older children to make a chart of the different colour combinations using coloured pens, for example, blue and yellow forming green, or red and blue to make purple.

Further ideas
■ Create coloured milk shakes using chopped fruit and food colourings.
■ Make a marble cake by lightly stirring together plain and chocolate sponge mixtures until the colours form a marble effect and then baking the mixture. Invite the children to ice and decorate the cake.
■ Talk to the children about rainbows. Show them pictures and invite them to make their own rainbow paintings.

What can you smell?

What you need
Water tray; water; essences such as almond, peppermint, lemon; perfume; flower petals; herbs such as mint, rosemary and thyme.

Preparation
Check that none of the children have allergies to any of the substances used.

What to do
Invite the children to smell the essences. Do they remind them of anything? Explain how essences are used to flavour foods.

Smell the herbs and talk about how they are used in cooking. Demonstrate how to crush the leaves between a finger and thumb to release the smell.

Talk about the children's experiences of perfume. Pass around the perfumes for the children to smell.

Smell the flower petals. Do they all have a smell? Explain how some flowers have a strong smell, while others have no smell at all.

Invite the children to smell the water in the water tray. Does it have any smell? Suggest that they choose one of the essences from the selection to add to the water tray. Once the children have played with the new solution for a while ask if they notice anything different about the smell of the water.

Ask the children to choose one of the herbs to scatter into the water and talk about changes to the smell. Continue by adding some flower petals and finally some perfume. Do the children like the resulting mixture of smells they have created?

Support and extension
Add one definite smell to the water, such as lemon or peppermint, before younger children begin to play. Do the children like the smell? Invite older children to create charts to record whether they like or dislike each smell. Head the charts 'essences', 'perfumes', 'petals' and 'herbs'.

Further ideas
■ Use tea bags, teapots, cups and jugs with the water so that the children can make imaginary cups of tea.
■ Make some 'smell boxes' using plastic tubs with holes in the lid so that the children can sniff the contents and guess what they are. Use strong scents such as grass, coffee and damp compost.

Slippery sculptures

What you need
Soap flakes; water; water tray; plastic cup.

What to do
Show the children the box of soap flakes and discuss what soap flakes are used for. Talk about the process of washing clothes at home. Check to see if there are any allergies.

Put some water into the water tray and ask the children to take turns to add a cup of soap flakes. Invite them to swish the mixture around after each cup is added and talk about the change of texture as the mixture thickens. Introduce appropriate vocabulary to support the children as they discuss how the mixture feels, for example, 'slippery', 'slimy', 'soft', 'smooth'.

Continue to add flakes until the mixture becomes more solid and can be moulded into peaks and mounds.

Allow time for the children to explore the mixture and to create sculptures by moulding it. Invite them to describe their creations.

Talk about the smell and appearance of the mixture. Does it remind the children of past experiences, such as playing in snow, bathtime or the smell of freshly washed clothes?

Support and extension
Prepare the mixture beforehand so that younger children can have fun playing with it and discovering more about how it behaves. Encourage older children to answer questions about their creations and to express their imaginary ideas through this medium. Introduce small-world characters to extend imaginary play.

Further ideas
■ Experiment with changing the colour of the mixture by adding food colouring to the water before adding the soap flakes.
■ Create a soapy dough by adding a tablespoon of liquid soap to a standard flour, salt and water play dough recipe.
■ Create a 'magic model mix' by mixing two cups of salt with two thirds of a cup of water and heating it until bubbles form. Then mix together one cup of cornflour and half a cup of water and stir this into the salt solution. Knead the resulting dough well. Make comparisons between the texture and appearance of plain dough and the soapy variety, and encourage the children to make models from each type of dough.

Changing colours

What you need
Crêpe paper in various colours; clear plastic bottles with screw tops; water tray; water; funnels.

Preparation
Check for any allergies to dyes. Cut the crêpe paper into long strips.

What to do
Ask each child to fill one of the bottles. Demonstrate how to use a funnel to make this task easier.

Invite the children to choose a strip of crêpe paper and dangle it into the neck of their bottle with the edge hanging over the top.

Show them how to screw the top back on tightly, giving them help if they need it.

Suggest that they shake their bottles up and down vigorously. What happens to the colour of the water? Can the children explain why these colour changes have occurred?

Ask the children to take the tops off their bottles and dangle a strip of crêpe paper of a contrasting colour into the bottle.

Screw the top on the bottle as before and shake it up. What has happened to the colour now?

Invite the children to pull the strips of crêpe paper out of their bottles. What has happened to them? Where has the colour gone? Introduce the word 'dye' and explain how the dye from the crêpe paper has coloured the water.

Suggest that the children take turns to pour the coloured water from their bottles into the water tray. Discuss the colour changes as they do so.

Support and extension
Invite younger children to wave strips of crêpe paper directly into the water tray rather than use bottles. Invite older children to try to create a specific colour, for example, by mixing together a bottle of blue and a bottle of red water to create purple water. Ask them to describe how they did so.

Further ideas
■ Mix powder paint to try to match the colours on colour charts you have collected from DIY stores.
■ Create mosaic patterns using blocks of colour cut from colour charts and invite the children to talk about the reasons for their colour choices.

Rangoli patterns

Time for a bath

This is how we wash our hands

(Tune: 'Here We Go Round the Mulberry Bush')

This is how we wash our hands, wash our hands, wash our hands,
This is how we wash our hands, so that we kill the germs.

First we turn the cold tap on, cold tap on, cold tap on,
First we turn the cold tap on, before we wash our hands.

Next we rub our hands with soap, hands with soap, hands with soap
Next we rub our hands with soap, so that we kill the germs.

Then we rinse them in the sink, in the sink, in the sink,
Then we rinse them in the sink, so that we kill the germs.

And last we have to dry them well, dry them well, dry them well
And last we have to dry them well, when they are nice and clean.

Sally Scott

Lost in the woods

Sophie and Ben, the two wriggling puppies, were having fun. They had found a hole in the garden fence and managed to wriggle through.

'Let's run', they barked.

They chased each other across the grassy field to the bumpy bridge, up and over the big hill, along the winding path and into the deep, dark woods. They yelped with excitement. Then Sophie began to pant. She flopped down under a big tree.

'Let's have a rest, Ben', she barked.

The two dogs stretched out and rested until they had stopped panting. Ben felt a rumble in his tummy.

'I'm hungry', he whined, 'Let's go home for some dinner, Sophie'.

Sophie leapt up.

'It's this way', she said, as she began to run along the path.

'No, Sophie, that way', growled Ben.

'This way', 'That way', 'This way', 'That way', they argued.

'Oh, Ben, we'll never get home if we keep arguing', yelped Sophie, 'Let's go this way for a few minutes, and if we still feel lost we'll turn around and go that way'.

'I agree', replied Ben. The two friends ran along the winding path.

'There's the big hill', barked Ben, 'We're going the right way. Let's climb up it'.

'No, let's run round it', said Sophie.

'Up', 'Round', 'Up', Round', they argued.

'Oh, Sophie, we'll never get home if we keep arguing', yelped Ben, 'I've got an idea. You guessed the right path so it's my turn to decide what to do.'

'I agree', answered Sophie. The two friends began to climb up the hill.

'There's the bumpy bridge', barked Sophie from the top of the hill, 'We're going the right way. The two friends began to run across the bumpy bridge.

They stood at the end of the bridge and stared across the grassy field.

'Look, Ben, it's our fence', said Sophie.

'And the hole is still there', answered Ben.

'I smell dinner', growled Ben.

'So do I', answered Sophie.

'Let's run' they barked, at exactly the same time.

The two friends had stopped arguing. They had better things to think about!

Jean Evans

The biggest dinosaur

Terry, the dinosaur, was getting bigger. Every day he grew bigger and bigger and bigger. Terry lived with the rest of the Tyrannosaurus Rex family in an enormous cave in the green valley. One day, Terry went outside to play with his brothers and sisters. 'Time for dinner', called dad from inside the enormous cave.

Terry's brothers and sisters ran inside and Terry went to follow them but, oh dear, as he pushed his growing body into the cave he became well and truly stuck.

'Help, help, I'm stuck', grunted Terry. His mum pushed and his dad pushed and his brothers and sisters pushed. What a struggle they had. Slowly, with a squeak and a creak, Terry began to move. 'Pop!', his body shot out of the cave onto the rocky ground outside.

'Oh, Terry', said his mum, 'You are too big to live with us any more. You must find somewhere else'.

Terry plodded off through the valley wondering what to do. On his way he met a stegosaurus.

'Hello, stegosaurus', he grunted, 'I'm too big for my family cave. Can you tell me what to do?'.

'I would use my bony plates to rub the sides of the cave and make it bigger', answered the stegosaurus.

'But I have no bony plates', grunted Terry, and on he went until he met a diplodocus.

'Hello, diplodocus. I'm too big for my family cave. Can you tell me what to do?'.

'I would use my long neck to pull the branches from the trees and build a new home', answered the diplodocus.

'But I have no long neck', grunted Terry, and on he went until he saw a pterodactyl flying overhead.

'Hello, pterodactyl', he grunted, 'I'm too big for my family cave. Can you tell me what to do?'.

'I would fly to a new valley and make a home there', answered the pterodactyl.

'But I have no wings and I cannot fly', grunted Terry, and on he went until he spotted a gap in the trees. Through the gap was the most enormous cave he had ever seen. He looked inside and it was empty.

'Just right for my new home' whispered Terry to himself.

That night Terry invited the rest of his family to a big party in the new home. And it was big enough for all of them!

Jean Evans

Letter home

Help!

I am lost.

My boat has landed on a tiny island.

I have drawn a map to help you to find me.

Please come and rescue me soon.

Love

....

Matching colours

(Tune: 'London Bridge')

(Make up a variety of verses with a different colour each time.)

Let's all point to something red,
Something red, something red,
Let's all point to something red,
With our fingers.

Sally Scott

Across the stones

Ten tall penguins

(Tune: 'Ten Green Bottles').

Ten tall penguins trying to keep cool,
Ten tall penguins trying to keep cool,
After one tall penguin dives down into a pool,
Only nine tall penguins are trying to keep cool.

(Continue singing verses, with one less 'penguin' each time, until all ten 'penguins' have jumped into the pool. Repeat the song again, while the children are sitting on the floor after diving, and invite them to stand up one at a time with each verse.)

One tall penguin hops out of the pool,
One tall penguin hops out of the pool,
After that tall penguin is feeling nice and cool,
Only nine tall penguins are swimming in the pool.

One more penguin hops out of the pool,
One more penguin hops out of the pool,
After that tall penguin is feeling nice and cool,
Only eight tall penguins are swimming in the pool.

(Continue until all ten penguins are standing up again.)

Sally Scott

Into the Ark

Race track

Pipe puzzle

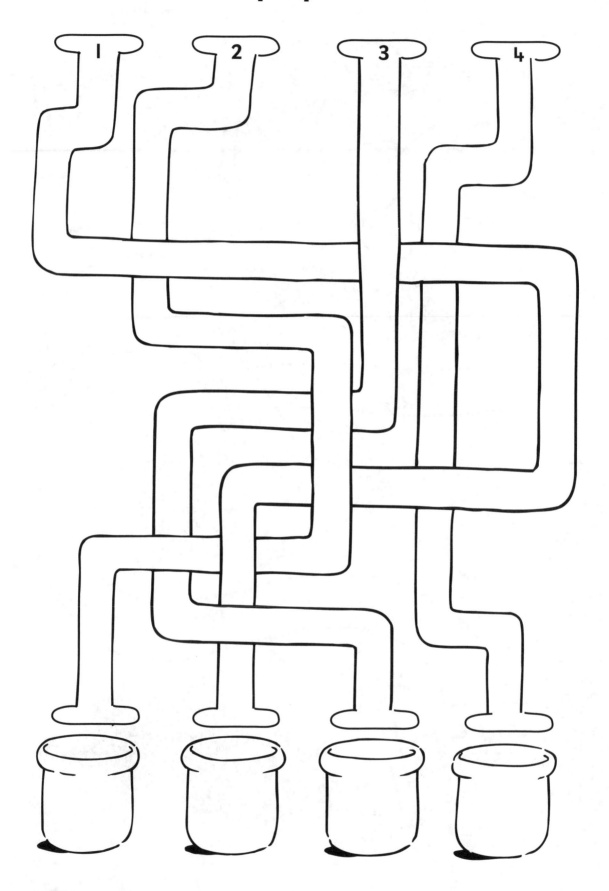

Down by the sea

(Tune: *Frère Jacques*)

Let's go paddling, let's go paddling
By the sea, by the sea,
Take your shoes and socks off, take your shoes and socks off,
Just like me, just like me.

Let's build castles, let's build castles,
By the sea, by the sea,
Use your spade and bucket, use your spade and bucket,
Just like me, just like me.

Let's go fishing, let's go fishing,
By the sea, by the sea,
Dip your net in rock pools, dip your net in rock pools,
Just like me, just like me.

*(Encourage the children to mime actions and to think up verses
of their own.)*

Sally Scott

Find the instruments